the new

Beagle

Ch. Tashwould Deja Vu, fifteen-inch dog (Ch. Torbay Final Fling ex Ch. Merry Song's High Spirit), the winner of multiple BIS, Groups and Specialties, including the 1995 and 1996 NBC Specialties. NBC Beagle of the Year, 1994, 1995, 1996, he is owned by Carroll Diaz and Kris Bloomdahl. *D. Kramer*

the new

Beagle

by
judith m. musladin, m. d.
a. c. musladin, m. d.
ada t. lueke

Second Edition

Illustrations by Ann Mackenzie
Contributions by Marie Shuart and
  Rosalind Hall

HOWELL
BOOK
HOUSE
New York

Howell Book House
A Simon and Schuster Macmillan Company
1633 Broadway
New York, NY 10019

Library of Congress Cataloging-in-Publication Data
Musladin, Judith.
    The new beagle/by Judith M. Musladin, A.C. Musladin, Ada T. Lueke: illustrations by Ann Mackenzie; contributions by Marie Shuart and Rosalind Hall. 2nd ed.
        p.   cm.
    Includes bibliographical references.
    ISBN 0-87605-028-3
    1. Beagles (Dogs)   I. Musladin, A.C. (Anton C.)   II. Lueke, Ada.
III. Title
SF429.B3M87 1998   97-39996
636.753'7--dc21   CIP

Manufactured in the United States of America

00 99 98   9 8 7 6 5 4 3 2 1

Book design: George McKeon

This book is dedicated to

SANDRA GROESCHEL

*Without your unmatched computer skills
and expert counseling,
this book would probably still be
in its birthing process.*

© Ann Mackenzie '88

Blueprint
of the Beagle

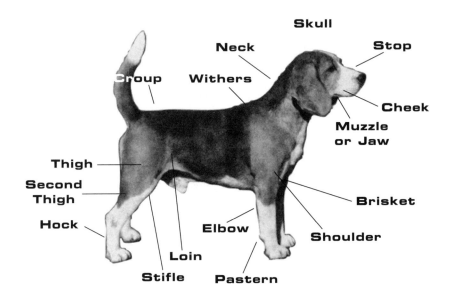

Skull

Neck

Stop

Croup

Withers

Cheek

Muzzle
or Jaw

Thigh

Second
Thigh

Brisket

Hock

Elbow

Shoulder

Loin

Stifle

Pastern

Contents

On the front cover: Ch. Lanbur Miss Fleetwood (headstudy), owned by Eddie
Dzuik and Jeffrey Slatkin. *Diane Quenell*
The Holly Hill Beagles turned out for a day's sport.
Kristine Kraeuter

Preface

The Beagle is one of the most popular purebred dogs in the United States. American Kennel Club statistics reveal that 56,946 Beagles were registered in 1996 and 57,063 in 1995. Of those, 380 achieved conformation championships; in Obedience, Beagles earned nineteen Companion Dog titles, six Companion Dog Excellent titles, two Utility degrees, six Tracking degrees and one became a Tracking Dog Excellent. In Agility, four Novice Agility titles, five Open Agility titles and one Agility Excellent title were earned. Not surprisingly, 457 completed their field championships.

Interestingly, despite an increase of almost 20,000 individual registrations since 1986, only the number of field champions (309 in 1986) has changed significantly.

The registration figures are staggering. What becomes of approximately 57,000 new Beagles each year?

Fortunately, the Beagle is a multipurpose breed and fulfills many of our human needs. It makes a loving friend, a splendid hunting companion and a fine obedience and conformation dog. It serves well with the Department of Agriculture by seeking out banned fruits and vegetables in airport baggage, visits convalescent hospitals as a "pet therapist," and even aids in termite detection!

This book, originally written for all who enjoy the Beagle and especially those who breed Beagles, has been revised to include changes occurring over the past eight years. Most chapters contain new information. We have chosen to keep David Sharp's "Starting and Training a Pack of Beagles" (Chapter 4) as originally published . . . it is a classic.

Bear with us in some of the technical discussion in the chapters on genetics and newborns. We feel the information is of particular importance in the breeding of Beagles and well worth absorbing.

Melody and Winston, members of the Australian Quarantine and Inspection Service, work the baggage carousels at international airports sniffing out items of prime quarantine concern: fruit, meat and other foodstuffs. This photo is actually the front side of a card given to incoming visitors to Australia. The reverse side resembles a postcard and bears a message from Melody and Winston introducing themselves, describing what they do and issuing a "friendly warning" about violating Australian quarantine regulations.

About the Authors

DRS. ANTON C. and **JUDITH M. MUSLADIN** acquired their first Beagle of field stock in 1959 and their first conformation puppy in 1961. Since then, both have been involved not only in breeding and showing their dogs, but also in associated Beagling activities. They have been members of, and have held various offices in, the Blossom Valley Beagle Club. Both are Supporting Members of the National Beagle Club of America. Judy served for three years as Director for the Supporting Membership from 1984 to 1987 and currently serves as Education Coordinator. Tony is currently approved to judge Beagles, Basenjis, Basset Hounds, Dachshunds and Whippets, and is Editor of the National Beagle Club's Supporting Membership newsletter.

For three years, together with Nadine Chicoine and David Hiltz, they published a breed magazine, *The American Show Beagle.*

Both Musladins are physicians—Tony is an orthopedist and Judy is a psychiatrist—and both are now retired. Their kennel name is The Whim's.

ADA T. LUEKE began her Beagling activities in 1967 and has bred and shown her Saga Beagles for thirty years. In addition, she has served as Bench Show Chairman and President of her local all-breed club, as well as a two-year stint as Director for the Supporting Membership of The National Beagle Club of America. Currently, she is Chairman of the Health and Genetic Committee.

Ada has a B.A. in Biology, with a special interest in genetics, and has worked in cellular research for some years. Collecting genetic information about our current family of conformation Beagles and advising on breeding choices is one of her many contributions.

Resumes of Marie Shuart and Rosalind Hall appear in the chapter on the Obedience Beagle. Some information from the contributors to the 1990 edition of *The New Beagle*, Nadine Chicoine, Warren Bushey, David Sharp, Herman Pyrkosz, Clifford and Edna Warren, Mary Powell and Trudi Reveira, has been used in this edition as well. We are very grateful to them all.

Richard P. Roth, current president of the National Beagle Club, with his Bare Cove Pack. *Mandy Bobbitt*

Acknowledgments

The authors wish to express their gratitude to the following for their assistance and contributions to this book:

Ann Mackenzie, an artist well-known for pen-and-ink dog and cat drawings marketed under the name "Tidings."

W. Jean Dodds, DVM, for her consultation on thyroid function.

Jack Pflock, DVM, Scotts Valley Veterinary Clinic, Scotts Valley, California, for his review of the dry-eye and cherry-eye material.

Helen Hamilton, DVM., Diplomate American College of Veterinary Internal Medicine, Santa Cruz Veterinary Hospital, Santa Cruz, California, for her review of the intersex material and comments on polyarteritis.

James Ticer, DVM, Diplomate American College of Veterinary Radiology, formerly with Santa Cruz Veterinary Hospital, Santa Cruz, California, for his help with the discussion of chondrodystrophy (epiphyseal dysplasia).

Alan Macmillan, DVM, Ph.D., Diplomate American College of Veterinary Ophthalmologists.

Michael J. Kelly, DVM, Diplomate American College of Internal Medicine, Main Street Animal Hospital, San Diego, California.

Patrick Gauvin, DVM, Chabot Veterinary Clinic, Hayward, California, for his correct diagnosis of chondrodystrophy in our current conformation family of Beagles.

Jacob Mosier, DVM, Professor Emeritus, Kansas State University Veterinary College, for his help in obtaining information about the "Chinese Beagle" Syndrome.

Donald Patterson, DVM, University of Pennsylvania Veterinary School, Philadelphia, Pennsylvania, for his help with intersex genetics.

Charles Miller, DVM, Scotts Valley Veterinary Clinic, Scotts Valley, California, for his help in researching some of the health and genetic problems in Beagles.

Pearl Baker, Editor of *Better Beagling*, for her wonderful collection of large-pack pictures.

Robert Slike of *Hounds & Hunting* magazine for his outstanding pictures of recent Brace Trials, as well as his patient explanations of the world of field trialing.

Gordon Burdick, AKC Field Trial Representative, for his time and valuable information.

Kristine Kraeuter and Wanda Borsa, of Holly Hills Registered Pack of Beagles, for their splendid collection of pictures and explanations.

Nadine Chicoine, Warren Bushey, David Sharp, Jr., Herman Pyrkosz, Clifford and Edna Warren, Mary Powell and Trudi Reveira for their contributions to the 1990 edition of *The New Beagle*, which served as the basis for this current edition.

Frank Lueke and Elizabeth Campbell for their encouragement and suggestions.

Seymour Weiss, Executive Editor, Howell Book House, for his patience, encouragement and support.

. . . And to all of you who have shared your pictures and information over the years.

the new

Beagle

Beagles, 1835.

The Southern Hound, an ancestor of the modern Beagle.

Orpheus, oil painting by Giovanni Castiglioni ("Il Grechetto"), ca 1650. *The Dog Book* by James Watson

The Beagle—Past and Present

"Pour down, then, a flood from the hills,
brave boys On the wings of the wind
The merry Beagles fly:
Dull sorrow lags behind
Ye shrill echoes reply,
Catch each flying sound,
And double our joys."

WILLIAM SOMERVILLE (1675–1742)

FROM THE MISTS OF TIME . . .

Early Man's association with wild canids probably began with the young being taken from dens and nurtured as pets or companions. Thereafter, in his search for food, man began to use the dog as an adjunct in hunting game. The scent hound used to track game probably evolved from breeding Bloodhound-type dogs to gazehounds, producing swiftness and a smaller size while retaining the keen sense of smell.

The Greek author Xenophon in the fourth century B.C. referred to small, Beagle-type dogs used to hunt hares on foot. Later, Romans in the conquest of Gaul and Britain are believed to have brought small hounds with them that interbred with the indigenous small hounds of Britain.

William the Conqueror, victor at the Battle of Hastings, brought from the continent to England the large, mostly white Talbot Hounds, which are considered to have contributed to the Southern Hound, a progenitor of the modern Beagle. During this same century, Edward the Confessor was noted to have hunted with small hounds identified as "kennettys."

The first Prince of Wales, later Edward II, wrote in letters of 1304 and 1305 that he had in his possession "low-legged harehounds of Wales who can well discover a hare after they find it sleeping and some of our running

1

dogs who can swiftly chase it," possibly referring to Basset- and Beagle-type hounds, respectively.

Later during the 1300s, there is mention in France of "rachys and brachys," small hounds brought from England by the Black Prince, son of Edward II, and John of Gaunt.

In any event, by the 1400s, small hounds were established not only in Britain but in France, Greece and Italy. According to Harold Schlintz in *Dog News*, the first traceable use of the word "Beagle" was around 1475 in the "Squire of Low Degree." The origin of the word is interesting. A word similar to "Beagle" is used in both French and Gaelic to mean "useless, of odd appearance, of little value." The smallest of scent hounds at that time, the Beagle had probably been bred for many years for amusement and/or hunting game of little significance, such as rabbits or hares.

THE BEAGLE IN ENGLAND

The Early Days

The little Beagle found favor with the British royal family. Chronicles of the reigns of Edward II and Henry VIII contain many references to the small hound. Described as being of diminutive size, the "glove Beagle" (tiny enough to be held in a gauntlet) was also called the "singing Beagle" for its melodious voice, which was so small in comparison to other hounds; efforts were even made to breed voices that would blend with one another.

Elizabeth I had a famous pack of tiny Beagles for the court's amusement. Nine inches in height at the shoulder, the "pocket Beagles" were carried behind the ladies of the court while on horseback. Paintings of the time show these Beagles to be short-legged with somewhat pointed noses.

Hunting hares with a pack of hounds was a popular sport for the country gentry of the day. Fox hunting had not yet achieved its eventual popularity, and the principal nobles and the Crown hunted deer with a large hound called the Buck Hound.

By the middle of the eighteenth century, fox hunting was beginning to attract the younger generation. The English Foxhound, most likely a product of the Buck Hound and the Beagle, was used for the faster, more exhilarating sport.

Due to the "vagaries of breeders" (*The Beagle in America and England*, by H.W. Prentice), two distinct types of hare-hunting hounds had evolved. The Southern Hound was slow-moving, with long ears and a deep voice; the North Country Beagle was quick and vigorous. In addition to these types, there was a smaller Beagle preferred by some for its small appetite. Though this latter type had a good nose for game, it tended to be playful and full of chatter. In short, an unreliable hunter! Obviously, there must have been hounds of various heights, shapes and colors.

Giant and Ringlet, two of Mr. Crane's famous pack of "pocket Beagles." *Dogs of Great Britain and America*

Lap Beagles, painting by Reinagle, ca 1800.

Blue Bell, a typical early Beagle. *Dogs of Great Britain and America*

With the advent of fox hunting, Beagles declined in popularity, and it is likely that the breed would have become extinct had it not been for the farmers and small landowners of the southern counties of England. It was the custom in that region to maintain packs of Beagles for the purpose of driving rabbits to the hunter's gun. Were it not for these Beagle packs and those in Ireland and Wales, there would have been no Beagles to participate in a revival of the breed.

The Beagle Club was founded in 1890 "to promote the breeding of Beagles for show and sporting purposes" (David Webster, The Australasian Beagle, 1986). The Beagle Club remained the only club representing the breed until 1961 when the Northern and Midlands Counties Beagle Club was formed, followed by another national club, the Beagle Association, and thereafter by six more regional clubs, including those in Scotland, Ireland and Wales. The Beagle Club is considered the parent club.

A Standard for the breed was published in 1895, and the first show by the Beagle Club took place in 1897.

The first Beagle champion, Belton Scornful, a bitch out of pack stock, was awarded in 1926. It was bred by a Mr. Roberts and owned by Mrs. Beaumont, who also owned the second Beagle champion, a son of Ch. Belton Scornful, who received its title in 1927.

During the period leading up to the Second World War, as well as during the war years, breeding and exhibiting seem to have had few enthusiasts. During the war, due to the great stresses on the British populace, these activities essentially came to a halt. However, a resurgence in breeding began in the late 1940s and continued thereafter at a remarkable pace.

Post-World War II to the 1990s

Barvae, one of Britain's leading Beagle kennels, owned by Gladys M. Clayton and daughter Patricia, began its illustrious career during the 1950s and has exerted a profound influence on the breed. Mrs. Clayton bred the first Beagle, Ch. Barvae Statute, owned by Mr. Fred Watson, to go Best in Show at an all-breed Championship Event. Barvae was also one of the earliest importers of American stock, acquiring Benroe Wrinkles in 1957.

Having had her first Beagle during the 1930s, Dolly Macro of Deaconfield Beagles continued a long love affair with the breed, and during the 1950s, bred to Ch. Barvae Statute—the beginning of a long line of very successful show and breeding stock.

The 1950s also saw the debut of the Appeline Kennel of Douglas and Carol Appleton, who began their line with a pack hound from the Warwickshire Beagles, Ch. Radley Triumph of Appeline, in 1951. In the late 1960s, the Appletons imported Am. & Eng. Ch. Appeline Validay Happy Feller, and in the 1980s, Am. & Eng. Ch. Pin Oaks Dynasty of Appeline.

"A British Family Portrait" (from left): Diana Spavin (Dialynne) with Ch. Soloman of Dialynne, Sylvia Tutchener (Beacott) with Ch. Fertrac Bramble of Beacott and Ch. Beacott Buckthorn and Mal Phillips (Fertrac) with Ch. Fertrac Anika and Ch. Fertrac Brandy. Ch. Beacott Buckthorn, a grandson of Ch. Dialynne Gamble, is the common thread behind the other hounds shown here.

Eng. Ch. Dialynne Tolliver of Tragband (Ch. Soloman of Dialynne ex Tragband Sweet Bird of Youth), Top Beagle in Great Britain, 1995, 1996, 1997; multiple Group and Best in Show winner at both Specialty and all-breed levels, owned by Andrew H. Brace. *Ron Willbie*

Veronica Bradley and K. Burgess (Dufosee) became a force in the world of Beagles and have continued to produce stock that is numbered among the top in Britain, as well as exports to various countries, including Australia, New Zealand and Latin America. Dufosee Bonnie Girl bred to the famous Ch. Dialynne Gamble produced multiple champions from several litters. A granddaughter brought Dufosee blood into Andrew Brace's Tragband line, producing very successful stock.

The Sutton family (Rossut) also began breeding Beagles during the 1960s and have produced dozens of champions accounting for numerous awards, multiple CCs and major awards at Championship shows—more Group and Best in Show awards than any other kennel in the breed. In 1982, Rossut obtained its first American import, Ch. Graadtre's Hot Pursuit of Rossut, which went all-breed Best in Show at its first show in England. Among its other get, it sired Andrew Brace's Ch. Too Darn Hot for Tragband, which was Britain's top winning bitch all breeds and Top Hound in 1984.

The Pinewood Kennel of Leonard and Heather Priestley bred a number of champions and also owned Ch. Southcourt Wembley Merryboy, which lists among its progeny Sylvia and Philip Tutchener's Ch. Beacott Buckthorn, which had an admirable show career, including a Hound Group First at Crufts in 1981.

Marion Spavin (Dialynne) based her line on Barvae stock and produced the great show winner and sire of multiple champions, Ch. Dialynne Gamble, identified by Andrew Brace in The *Australasian Beagle,* 1986, as "the Father of the Contemporary Beagle." Few United Kingdom Beagle kennels do not have Gamble in their background.

Ch. Dialynne Gamble was by Ch. Appeline Validay Happy Feller, an American import, out of Ch. Dialynne Nettle, a granddaughter of Mrs. Spavin's first homebred champion, Dialynne Huntsman. As with the other leading United Kingdom Beagle kennels, Dialynne is well-represented by show and breeding stock in many other countries.

Other Beagle kennels that have produced outstanding breed representatives over the years include Thelma Grey's Rozavel, Annasline (Judith Ireland), Raimex (Diana Brown), Forrardon (Pamela Harris), Cornevon (Gibson), Jesson (Eades) and Bayard (Peak). In Scotland, outstanding breed representatives include Korwin (Christine Watson), Norcis (Eleanor and Frank Bothwell) and Mistylaw (Betty Whyte).

David Webster, of the Webline Beagles, warrants special mention as an important force in English Beagledom. After having been a committee member of the Beagle Club for a number of years, Mr. Webster became the Honorary Secretary of the organization in 1965, holding that critical position for well over the next two decades. More recently, he has been serving as a vice president of the Beagle Club. He has been a championship show judge for many years.

A Working Section of the Beagle Club was established in 1963, with the early meetings being live hunts but more recently drag hunts. As of the late 1980s, ninety Beagles had gained Working Certificates, including twenty show champions. These certificates acknowledge that the recipients had been "found to enter to hare, give tongue and be free from riot" and are signed by two qualified judges, usually Masters of Hounds or Huntsmen (David Webster, *The Australasian Beagle*, 1986).

THE BEAGLE IN AMERICA

Early Beaglers and Their Dogs

Prior to the importation of pack dogs from England in 1876 by General Richard Rowett of Carlinville, Illinois, various types of dogs were identified as "Beagles": large, straight-legged ones, "bench-legged Beagles," as well as Bloodhound, harrier and terrier types. The bench-legged variety was particularly prevalent and in favor at that time with breeders in southern Pennsylvania, Delaware and Maryland.

General Rowett's careful selection of tricolored hounds produced dogs of good conformation and hunting ability. As a result, his stock was in great demand and was incorporated into the breeding stock of many other lines that also featured English imports during the 1880s and 1890s, including those of Charles Turner, J.M. Dodge and Norman Elmore.

After General Rowett's death, his stock was incorporated into the breeding programs of Pottinger Dorsey and C. Staley Doub of Maryland. Hiram Card (Blue Cap), who favored a blue-ticked or mottled color and whose stock was descended from English imports, also bred into Rowett stock, producing excellent field dogs with keen noses and good voices. Edward Marshall of Michigan also used the Rowett strain to produce his Middletown hounds, known for their clean necks and shoulders.

J.M. Dodge also availed himself of Rowett stock. His famous duo of Rattler, which was by Charles Turner's import Warrior out of General Rowett's Rosy, and Belle (Darwin ex Millay) had illustrious show careers, with Rattler never failing to take first place and Belle having three firsts.

One of the outstanding Beagles of the late 1800s was Frank Forest, a product of Rowett linebreeding by George Reed of Vermont and shown with great success by his owner, Mr. Perry of Massachusetts, both in the field and on the bench.

Frank Forest, an important early American stud.

Rattler and Belle, owned by J.M. Dodge. Rattler, by Charles Turner's Warrior ex General Rowell's Rosy, won first place at Philadelphia, Boston, St. Louis, Rochester and Ann Arbor in 1879. Belle won first place in Philadelphia and Boston in 1879.

First Field Trial of the National Beagle Club; November 3, 1890. *The Beagle in America and England*, H.W. Prentice

Portions of a wonderful letter from George Reed to Staley Doub after the New York show of 1897 follow:

Now Post asked for dogs for Special No. 1. In comes Thornwood, Truman, Hector, Florist, Ring Leader, Roy K and Frank Forest. Ringleader had already beat Frank and Roy K, Lonely II, Oronsay Matron and old Champion Lonely, and the fun went on.

Now, boys, I was ready for this procession. I was with Harker five minutes before they were called, and Old Bill (William Saxby) was to come to the bench when they wanted him and let me know.

I had the rough hair on his shoulder flat, the rest of the body and coat I let alone. I took off his collar and put on a small but firm fish line, as I have noticed a collar presses the skin back, making his shoulders look loaded. You could not see the cord. It was under the hair, and I snapped a chain on the cord; so here we all go around the ring for ten minutes. Lonely II bothered Harker, as he could smell her as she was in heat.

The first ones to go into the corner were Hector, Frank, Roy K, Truman, then old Lonely, then Thornwood and Robino, then Matron. This left Ringleader, Florist and Harker. Then dear old Pard, I needed all my nerve, for I could hear and feel my heart beat.

Post ordered us to the bench in the middle of the ring. First Harker on the left, then Florist and Ringleader, then I reached down and unsnapped the chain from the cord and dear old Harker stood like a statue, legs well under him, brush carried gaily.

First Post looked Ringleader over, then Florist, then he told the great Joe Lewis with his great Ringleader to take Ringleader to the corner with the rest. Staley, I did not dare look up or away from Harker for fear I would smile. Now he takes Harker and the dear old boy stood up like a major. I snapped the chain on the collar and gave him a run across the ring to show his motion and back on the bench, and boys, I done my level best. I drew my hand down over the fore leg to the feet, for I knew if Post looked at his feet I could beat Florist there. I had a small piece of Vermont horse (hoof) in my hand and Harker knew it was there. At last Mr. Post awarded me the ribbon enclosed in this letter, and it was over.

My hand trembles now to think of it. The feat had been accomplished. Harker had won over the four cracks, Ringleader, Lonely, Frank Forest and Roy K. All the boys clapped their hands; first to congratulate me by shaking hands was Mr. Kernochan, and on leaving the ring, I raised my hat to the bunch. It took me some time to put on his collar for tears were running like the devil, boys, and I felt good. Staley, you say you boys felt good. Do you think you can imagine my feelings? No, I know you can't half. Think what I had been through since I saw Harker was in the wrong class. I had made this victory for my dear Maryland friends, not for myself, and dear old Maryland friends, if it has given you boys any pleasure I am glad, for the first among my heart friends are you boys.[1]

[1]*Prentice, H.W.* The Beagle in America and England. *1920.*

George B. Post, Jr., the judge of the day, was one of the early and successful exhibitors of Beagles. His stock, too, was of Rowett breeding.

The early American show Beagles were of a rangier type, often pied or mottled in markings, as were the best English hunting strains, and ranged in size from "toy to sixteen inches" in height.

Heated debate over what constituted a proper Beagle flourished in the press of the 1880s. *Forest and Stream* and *American Field* published letters (most authors signing themselves as "Zim," "Briar," "Rusticus," or some other sporting *nom de plume*) in which size, dwarfism, long backs, cobbiness of back, bench versus field type, pedigrees, color, the quality of American Beagles over the English, styles of hunting and a host of other topics were chewed over endlessly. There was even a reference to the famous imported Ch. Ringwood that actually described it as a caricature of a Bloodhound!

As you can readily gather, heated debate has long been a part of the Beagle world.

The Founding of the National Beagle Club

The American-British Beagle Club, formed by Beagle breeders in the Philadelphia area, drafted the first Standard for the breed in January 1884, which—with the establishment of the American Kennel Club—became the first official AKC Standard for the breed.

The National Beagle Club was established in the late 1800s for the dual purpose of holding Field Trial Events and improving field qualities as well as type. When the club applied for admission to the American Kennel Club, permission was denied, because the American Beagle Club, as the American-English Beagle Club became known, refused to sanction its admission. Despite the denial, the new club continued its plans and in short order merged with the American Beagle Club to create the National Beagle Club of America (NBC).

Early in its existence as the National Beagle Club of America, a proposal to strike from its constitution references to improvement of conformation on the bench was voted down. The club was clearly on record in support of promoting function and type. The Standard was revised in 1900 to increase emphasis on running gear (legs and feet).

With the establishment of the National Beagle Club of America, it became a tradition "that a Bench Show is held during the fortnight of the trials, generally on a Sunday, to which the countryside is invited and entertained at lunch" (Lentilhon, Eugene. *Forty Years of Beagling in the United States*. New York: E.P. Dutton and Company, 1921).

The first National Beagle Club Field Trial was held at Hyannis, Massachusetts in November 1890. However, due to poor terrain, subsequent trials were moved to New Hampshire. The first National Beagle Club Specialty

Show was held in 1891. Initially, classes were divided by varieties, but first-place class winners, both thirteen- and fifteen-inch, competed for Winners awards and championship points. Generally, the larger Beagle was awarded the points during that period. It was not until 1928 that Beagles were shown in two totally separate varieties with points awarded in both.

Bench, Pack and Field

The Bench-Beagle type was commonly derogated in the Field Trial press of the day. In response, James Kernochan began in 1896 to import proven hunting hounds from English packs, adding the hound head and body as well as legs and feet of a good Beagle; these imports were instrumental in setting the Beagle type of today. Mr. Kernochan's Hempstead Hounds, the Windholme stock of Harry Peters and the Rock Ridge Beagles of William A. Rockefeller were the most successful in early shows. All these dogs also worked in the field and performed well.

English imports, such as Eng. Ch. Stoke Place Sapper, also proved themselves both on the bench and in the field by winning high honors.

Until 1912, Field Trials were held on cottontail and only rarely on New England hare. After that date, pack-on-hare clubs established the Beagle's endurance in the field on larger game.

From the early 1900s to the 1920s, shows were dominated by entries from the outstanding packs of the day—not only Windholme and Rockridge, but also Sir Sister, Waldingfield, Wolver, Somerset and Wheatley packs. Ch. Windholme's Bangle, a fifteen-inch bitch, became the first Best in Show Beagle, taking the top prize at the December 1901 Ladies Kennel Association of America Event held at the first Madison Square Garden in New York City.

The 1940s and 1950s saw the rise of Kinsman (Lee Wade), Sogo (Clinton Callahan), Liseter (Mrs. A. du Pont), C.S. (Charles Schultze), Johnson's (Ed Johnson), Forest (Ed Jenner), Johjean (Mr. and Mrs. John Refieuna), Validay (Mr. and Mrs. Val Davies), Jacobi (E. Jacobi), White Acres (Margaret White), Meadoglo (Elsie Johnson) and Ralph's (Donald Ralph). Pedigrees of the dogs of that period contain names of pack and field dogs, and many were dual-purpose hounds. Ch. Duke Sinatra and Ch. Thornridge Wrinkles were two of the most widely-known dogs of that period. Ralph's and White Acres continue to breed and exhibit at the present time.

The years since the early 1960s have seen a veritable explosion in the number of conformation Beagle breeders throughout the United States and Canada as interest in the breed has flourished. Based on some of the lines that were prominent in earlier decades, breeders who have carried out more extensive breeding programs include Alpha-Centauri, Bayou Oaks, Buglair, Busch's, Chardon, Colegren, Daf-i-Dale, Dismal Creek, Elsy's, Felty's, Foyscroft, Fulmont, Junior's, Just-Wright, Kings Creek, Lanbur,

Meadowcrest, Merry Song, Navan's, Page Mill, Pickadilly, Pine Lane, Pin Oaks, Pixshire, Plain & Fancy, Shaw's, Starbuck, Starcrest, Sun Valley, Sure Luv, Swan Lake, Tarr Hill, Teloca, The Whim's, Wagon Wheels, Wilkeep, Whiskey Creek, Wishing Well, Wright-Eager, Wynborne's and Yaupon Row. Many of these breeders are active today.

Other breeders who have had an influence on the breed, although with limited breeding programs, include Alamo, Beagle Chase, Beowulf, Birchwood, Boudje, Brantwood, Buttonwood, Chrisette, Daisyrun, Densom, Dreams Of, Downey, Eagle Ridge, Englandale, Fran-Ray, Gar-Rene, Graadtre, Greenwood, Hare Hollow, Harnett, Hayday, Hemlock, Hollypines, Jabrwoki, Jam's, Jo-Lee, Kamelot, Lacoste, Lee's, Lohenbru, Loverly, Meadowland, Nieland, Pacific, Perky's, O'Boy, Rancho Glen, R.D.'s, Rowdy's, Saga, Shadowland, Skyline, Southspring, Stonebridge, Tanbark, Tashwould, Terwillegar, The Tavern's, Tooker, Torbay, Whisper, Wits End, Vijam, Vinla, Windy-roc and Yarra-belle.

Four of the registered Beagle packs—Bedlam, Glenbarr, Holly Hill and Sir Sister—have performed successfully both in the field and in the show ring.

In the last thirty years, many Beagles have been awarded multiple all-breed Bests in Show. Some of them are Ch. Kings Creek Triple Threat (Marcia and Tom Foy), Ch. The Whim's Buckeye (Dr. and Mrs. A.C. Musladin), Ch. Starbuck's Hang 'Em High (David and Linda Hiltz), Ch. Busch's Nuts to You of Brendons (Mr. and Mrs. Bill Busch), Ch. Teloca Patches Littl' Dickens (Wade Burns, Jon Woodring and Marie Shuart), Ch. Navan's Triple Trouble Rick (Virginia Flowers), Ch. Keith's Wilkeep Nicodemus (Barbara Cosgrove) and Ch. Page Mill Upset the Applecart (Greta Haag). The 1990s have seen a fresh crop of multiple all-breed Bests in Show Beagles, including Ch. Dismal Creek's Li'l Big Man (Bruce Tague and Mark Lister), Ch. Lanbur Miss Fleetwood (Eddie Dzuik, Wade Burns and Jon Woodring), Ch. Bayou Oaks Cappucino (Alyce and Richard Gilmore), Ch. Terwillegar's Hit the Roof (Jane Lloyd), Ch. Tashwould Deja Vu (C. Diaz and C. Bloomdahl) and Ch. Whiskey Creek's Headliner (M. Delia and M. Sager).

The number of shows has proliferated at a rapid rate, and combined with the ease of air transportation, it is quite probable that previous records and those of the present top-winning Beagles will continue to fall.

As can be seen by the number of Beagle conformation prefixes, there has been a definite shift away from large, wealthy kennels dominating the shows to myriad small breeding programs. From the 1800s to the early 1950s, Beagles competed in the field and in the conformation ring concurrently. Now, as we approach the millenium, most conformation Beagles have never even seen a rabbit, much less run one. Many of the current breeders live in or near metropolitan areas with kennel facilities ranging from separate small outbuildings equipped with runs to basement housing for the dogs and even to the small operation within the main residence itself. Breeding for nose, voice and tracking skills has been replaced by breeding for good looks and sweet dispositions.

For breeders with limited space, the selection of stock to be retained for showing and breeding has to be made early. Breedings, perforce, are limited. However, as a result, test breeding takes a back seat to breeding for good show prospects. Reliable information about genetic and temperament problems has never been more important.

Conditioning your Beagle today takes place not in the field but in backyards, school grounds after hours, city parks, behind bicycles or joggers and on treadmills.

Beagle Clubs

Beagle Clubs sponsoring Specialties come and go. Although licensed Field Trial clubs number in the hundreds, AKC-licensed clubs holding annual conformation Specialties now number seven: National Beagle Club of America (the parent club), Aldie, Virginia; Blossom Valley Beagle Club, San Jose, California; Phoenix Arizona Beagle Club, Phoenix, Arizona; San Jacinto Beagle Club, Pasadena, Texas; Southern California Beagle Club, Los Angeles area, California; Wisconsin Beagle Club, Ft. Atkinson, Wisconsin and Southern New York Beagle Club, generally held with the Westchester Kennel Club show. During the last fifteen to twenty years, four venerable clubs—Bay State, Chicago, Northern California, and San Joaquin Beaglers—have either disbanded or dropped their annual Specialties.

Most of the currently licensed clubs also hold Field Trials and have offered annual Specialty Shows for a number of years. Some are the product of a small nucleus of conformation Beaglers joining receptive established Field Trial clubs to undergo the licensing process required by the AKC to eventually hold a Specialty Show. Not every Field Trial club is inclined to be bothered with conformation Beaglers. Fortunately, there are some, so it can be done!

Two new clubs composed of energetic and devoted Beaglers have been formed during the late 1990s: the Columbia-Willamette Beagle Club, Oregon-Washington, has been licensed by the AKC and is scheduled to hold its first Specialty Show in 1998, whereas the Rocky Mountain Beagle Club, Colorado, is undergoing its prelicensing process. These clubs will not only offer Specialty Shows but will also contribute to educating Beaglers and the general public about the breed.

Institute Farm, Aldie, Virginia, home of the National Beagle Club. *Rene Chicoine*

Trailer, owned by General Rowett, ca 1880. *The Beagle in America and England*, H.W. Prentice

Institute Farm

In 1916, James W. Appleton (president of the NBC, 1910-1942), Harry Peters, and George B. Post, Jr. (the latter two, directors of the American Kennel Club), Chetwood Smith, Ted Lucas, H.C. Phipps of Wheatley Beagles and C. Oliver Iselin (president of the NBC, 1942-1971) formed the Institute Corporation and purchased the 400-acre Institute Farm in Aldie, Virginia as the home of NBC activities.

This wooded property, located about thirty miles west of Washington, D.C., had once been part of Oak Hill, home of President James Monroe. In 1854, a large three-and-one-half story stone and stucco building was erected for the Loudoun County Agricultural Institute and Chemical Academy. The first agricultural school in the Commonwealth of Virginia, its students and faculty pioneered agricultural experimentation.

The site, with its house, provided good ground conditions for hunting and sleeping quarters for eager hunters. Perimeter fencing to keep the Beagles from straying, kennel facilities and log cabins to afford additional sleeping accommodations completed the project. This then became the locus for Pack Trials, both for Beagles and Basset Hounds, and Brace Trials—a tradition that prospers even today.

In 1981, Institute Farm was placed on the National Registry of Historic Places and Virginia Landmarks Registry to insulate it from suburban creep from Washington, D.C. The Loudoun Agricultural Chemical Institute Foundation, Inc., was formed in 1986 to serve as a fund-raising vehicle for restoration of the building and grounds to the original nineteenth-century state. Considerable restoration and upgrading of the building has been carried out, and the work continues to the present. Acquiring adjacent properties is also under consideration.

The early National Beagle Club's emphasis on both field and conformation changed over the years as interest in conformation waned. By 1936, the task of administering the increasing number of Field Trial clubs and activities became an impossible burden, and a separate governing body, the Beagle Advisory Committee, was established.

In 1970, a small group of conformation Beaglers, also regular members of the NBC, with the encouragement of the Secretary, Morgan Wing, held the first National Beagle Club Specialty in many years at Aldie. Virginia Coleman, Evelyn Droge, Louise Marter and Archie Chapman put on eight successful annual Specialty Shows.

Growing pressure for representation by conformation Beaglers in the NBC eventuated in the establishment of a second classification of membership, the Supporting Membership, for those interested in conformation. Through the pioneering work of Nadine Eaton Chicoine during the late 1970s, the Supporting Membership was granted permission in 1980 to draw up its own bylaws governing Specialty Show activities and providing for the election of a Supporting Membership Director to serve on the Board of the NBC.

Ch. Lanbur Miss Fleetwood, thirteen-inch bitch (Ch. Lanbur The Company Car ex Ch. Altair's Lanbur Lacy J), multiple BIS and Group winner; BOB NBC Specialty, 1991 and 1993; NBC Beagle of the Year, 1992 and 1993. Owned by Eddie Dzuik and Jeffrey Slatkin.

Ch. White Acres I Think I Can, fifteen-inch dog (Ch. Daf-I-Dale's Willy R Wonti, CD ex Ch. White Acres Designer Jam), owned by White Acres Kennels, reg.

The year 1981 saw the inception of a regular rotation schedule for the Specialty Show throughout the United States, returning to Aldie every fifth year. This step was taken to permit greater participation by Beaglers based away from the East Coast. Show venues away from Aldie are voted on by the Supporting Members, based on applications submitted by individual NBC Supporting Members or members of regional Beagle Clubs. These members or clubs serve as hosts to the NBC Specialty and, in some instances, also organize a separate Specialty of their own to be held in conjunction with the NBC Specialty.

The National Beagle Club of America lists 483 Regular Members and 208 Supporting Members as of November 1997. Activities sponsored by the parent club include spring and fall Basset and Beagle Pack Trials, Brace Trials, an annual Specialty Show and, most recently, a Triple Challenge weekend at Aldie. The 1987 centennial celebration of the club's founding provided clear evidence of an active club committed to its original purpose.

With the passage of time, a shift has occurred away from the dual-purpose hound of the late 1800s and early 1900s to the breeding of Beagles for a specific function: conformation, brace, large and small pack and gundog. Because of this shift, Beagles in these categories seem in some instances to represent different breeds. However, within the registered Beagle packs, as well as in the more recent gundog movement, there is increasing interest in combining the qualities of a good working hound with the beauty of the conformation Beagle.

THE BEAGLE IN OTHER LANDS

Beagles are popular not only in Great Britain and the United States, but in many countries in both the Northern and southern hemispheres. English and/or American stock have provided the foundation for the breeding programs in many of these countries.

Canada

Canadian Beagles and Beaglers have been closely identified with their counterparts in the United States for many years. Some of the earlier kennels—Phillip Jacobi (Jacobi's) in Eastern Canada, for example—from the 1940s to the 1960s tended toward close inbreeding, as did Bob McKillop (Meri-mac) in Edmonton during the 1950s, basing his breeding on Jacobi stock. Another Beagle breeder, Donna James (Briarpatch), also based her line on Jacobi stock and showed successfully for a number of years.

Subsequent Beagle breeders began to incorporate American stock. Gwen Marotte (Yarra-belle) in British Columbia combined her Australian stock, based on English bloodlines, with American, initially The Whim's, but later also Starcrest and Challenge Kennels. Jane Lloyd of Alberta has developed her Terwillegar Beagles based on Yarra-belle stock (combining Australian and

Am. & Can. Ch. Terwillegar's Hit the Roof, fifteen-inch dog (Ch. Page Mill On The Road Again ex Ch. The Whim's Raise The Roof), multiple BIS, Group and Specialty winner. Sire of ten champions. Top Beagle in Canada in 1992, 1993, 1994. Owned by Mrs. G.R. Lloyd. *Mikron*

American bloodlines) and The Whim's bloodline, as well as other Canadian and American lines, with considerable success.

More of the "old-timers," as well as recent breeder/exhibitors, include Lori Bulmer (Meriadoc Beagles), Ray Hornbostel (Buttonwood), Bill and Susan Gear (Lenergie), Holly Fitzharding (Bakerstreet), Becky Kinsey (Goodsir), Kevin and Eileen Shupenia (Jackpot), Dennis and Donna Somers (Densom) and Shirley Winslow (Lenwin).

The Beagle Club of British Columbia, based in Victoria, was formed through the efforts of Beth Breingan and Marlene Caskey (Breigayt); it held its first annual Specialty in October 1996.

Continental Europe

SWEDEN

Sweden's Beagle Club was founded in 1953 by a group of Beaglers primarily interested in hunting. Sweden is one of the few countries with breed clubs that require a show champion to also have a full Field Trial Championship. The dichotomy of Bench and Field Beagles seen the United States does not exist. American and British imports have played an important role in current Swedish lines, including Am., Dk. and Int. Ch. Seven Hills Black Gold, owned by I.C. Christensen, Denmark. Black Gold qualified as an international champion by way of a Field Trial in Germany, proving that even an American show dog can work in the field! Its grandson, Dk. Ch. Black Gold II, out of an English bitch, Pinewood Courtesy, was bred by Catherine Linde and was imported by the Hansens (Parup Kennels) into Denmark where he proved to have a profound influence on the breed. Imports from England included stock from Rozavel, Annasline and Bodigga, which also had American antecedents.

DENMARK

Next-door neighbor, Denmark, has become an enthusiastic supporter of Beagles since they were first introduced in 1963 from Sweden and Finland. Over the following years, more imports came from England, Scotland, and the United States as well. Emphasis on show stock has been on the larger Beagles, generally between fourteen and fifteen inches. In contrast to Sweden, no Field or Pack Trials are held, and as a consequence, a field championship is not required.

The first major Danish breeder was I.C. Christensen (O'Connic's), who founded the Danish Beagle and Basset Club and based his line mainly on American stock. Other breeders who have contributed significantly to the Danish Beagle of today are Tove Pitzner (Minette), Nina and Finn Vinther (Daisy Hill), Kristian and Bodil Hansen (Parup), Anna Sofie Gothen (Red Baron), the late Claus Sorensen (Magic Noire), Inger and Flemming Brodersen (Famous Joker), Annette and Jesper Pedersen (Gold Line), Jytte French (French), Jess and Christa Schmidt (Dazzler), Ulla Hvidberg (Ulradi) and Karen and Marianne Ulrich (Susquatch). These breeders have thoughfully combined various imported stock as well as breeding among the Danish kennels themselves, producing some excellent representatives of the breed.

GERMANY

Beagles in Germany, as in other European countries, can measure up to sixteen inches at the withers. Control of the breed is closely observed by the German Beagle Club (BCD), which publishes an annual stud book; listed for each dog are parentage, findings on hip x-rays (hip dysplasia scores), show records of the individual dog, get produced and so on. No dogs can be bred before x-rays are taken to determine the status of the hips in keeping with a German Kennel Club (VDH) regulation. After a successful breeding and whelping, the health of the dam and litter are checked at eight weeks after birth by a veterinarian and the club's breed warden. The pups are tattooed with the stud book number and registered by the BCD. Any abnormalities in the litter are noted, and any puppies with congenital life-threatening defects are euthanized.

FINLAND

Beagles intended for use in the field have been bred in Finland for many years, but show Beagles are relative newcomers. During the past twenty-five years or so, however, Eeva Resko (Daragoj) has developed her line based on imports from Great Britain, the United States, Australia, Scandinavia and Canada.

Her stock, in turn, has been exported to other Scanadinavian countries, as well as South America, Canada and the United States, exerting a significant influence on Beagles in these far-flung regions of the dog-showing world.

THE NETHERLANDS

The history of Beagles in the Netherlands appears to be relatively brief. With the exclusion of one or possibly two dedicated breeders, Dutch activity is based on pet-quality production to satisfy a general public demand. Apparently, breeders of better quality have "come and gone" over the years with some frequency.

However, Holland does have Baroness van der Borch tot Verwolde (Sergeant Pepper Beagles), who has in essence carried the banner for Beagles for about thirty years, successfully producing many fine hounds. Her winning stock is based on imports from the United States, Canada, Britain and New Zealand, blending various strains that combine beauty and character. Some of her dogs are proficient in field work as well as in the show ring—not only in the Netherlands, but also in other Western European countries.

Down Under

Beagles bred in Australia and New Zealand are primarily derived from English lines, with some more recent introduction of American breeding primarily via American exports to Britain. Exports from the U.S. must first undergo a four-month quarantine in Britain and a one-month residency in Hawaii, if that route is followed, with additional quarantine of four months prior to entry into either Australia or New Zealand. Quarantine is imposed on dogs passing through the United Kingdom as well. The attendant high cost has probably limited the number of exports from the United States. Possible changes in quarantine regulations resulting from the opening of the "Chunnel" between France and Britain may eventually affect import activity to the Southern Continent. As this book goes to press, it's too soon to know, but it's interesting to speculate on the potential ramifications.

The introduction of English and American stock during the past twenty-five to thirty years into the previously-established Australian and New Zealand strains has produced Beagles of more moderate size. The Australian and New Zealand Standard follows in essence the English Standard of "desirable" height between thirteen and sixteen inches. English kennels that have had a marked influence on the conformation of today's Australian and New Zealand Beagles include Rozavel, Raimex, Dialynne, Dufosee and Annasline, with Aus.& N.Z. Ch. Annasline Fanfare having a particularly significant effect on the breed. From the United States by way of England came Am. & Aus. Ch. Page Mill Oscar and Aus. Ch. Page Mill Lucky Lady, which contributed their genes primarily to the Torbay Beagles of Lesley Funnell Hiltz and the Manahound Beagles of Liz Whitcher Rosback. Western Australian Beagles have been influenced by Truda and Cyril Mawbry's (Clarion Beagles) importation of the American-bred Aus. Ch. Lees Pennon from the United Kingdom. In 1994, Am. Ch. Starbuck Torbay Colours, sired by Am. Ch. Starbuck's Hang 'em High (The Whim's and Elsy's lines) was imported into New Zealand.

Presently, Australia and New Zealand have a total of seven Beagle Clubs: Beagle Club, Inc (established 1972) and Auckland Beagle Club of New Zealand, Beagle Club of Tasmania, Beagle Club of South Australia, Beagle Club of New South Wales (formed 1946), Western Australia Beagle Club (founded 1985) and Beagle Club of Victoria (founded 1964) in Australia. The clubs offer various services, including championship shows as well as matches, handling classes, Beagle Walks and hunts under the direction of a huntmaster and staff.

National Beagle Championship shows have been held in 1985 and 1992, hosted by regional clubs, with plans to continue these shows about every three years in the future. Entries have come from all seven Australian states and New Zealand.

South Africa

Beagles in South Africa are relatively limited in number, probably as a result of the political and economic situation that isolated the country for many years, limiting importation as well as showing and breeding. Judging follows the English system, requiring five Challenge Certificates (CCs) to obtain a championship. Challenge Certificates won before age nine months do not count, and one CC must be won after eighteen months of age.

Show stock in South Africa is primarily English, with a few from Australia and a rare one from the United States and Germany. Beagles were first exhibited in South Africa in 1883, but the first record of a champion was not until 1956! Imports of note were from the Barvae and Cannybuff Kennels of England. The Beagle Club of Transvaal was founded in 1980.

Japan

Conformation Beagles in Japan (ranked tenth of all breeds in 1995) are primarily of American origin and have been exported from the United States during the past twenty to twenty-five years. Japan currently has no size limitation, but the smaller dogs that measure about thirteen inches are highly favored by most breeder/exhibitors. However, some breeders apparently have given some thought to the increased use of stock in the fifteen-inch variety to maintain breed type and improve quality.

Latin America

Latin America has become a veritable "hotbed" of Beagle activity during the past thirty to thirty-five years, particularly in Brazil, Argentina and Columbia. As in other parts of the world, imports from the United Kingdom and the United States, and later from Finland, have formed the gene pool that is resulting in contemporary show-quality animals as the twentieth century draws to a close.

BRAZIL

Beagles in Brazil are one of that country's most popular breeds, captivating a large number of breeder/exhibitors over the years following introduction. Early kennels were Goldpulver (Arthur Luis Gerhard), based in Rio de Janeiro, and Dreamland (Paulo and Vera Lucia Costa) of Sao Paulo, the latter bringing in show stock from the United States in the 1970s. Another kennel based on Goldpulver breeding, Glenrose, introduced bloodlines, primarily Dialynne, from England, as well as stock from Pumar, an Argentinian kennel, and from the well-known Johjean's Beagles in America.

Other breeders appeared on the scene in rapid succession during the 1970s and 1980s, basing their lines on British and American stock. Camp's Kennel of Jose Luis Pinto Moreira in Sao Paolo combined The Whim's stock from the United States with representatives of various English lines, including, once again, Dialynne. Dr. Pinto Moreira eventually handed on his breeding stock to Alberto Bonfiglioli Neto (Sto Alberto Kennel), who has continued to actively breed and exhibit, incorporating White Acres and The Tavern's imports from the United States. A fellow Beagler in Sao Paolo, Marcelo Tuck Schneider, founded the Bangor Kennel and brought in stock from the United States based on the King's Creek line, but also added The Whim's, Johjean and, more recently, Daf-I-Dale and Starbuck/Torbay bloodlines from the United States, as well as Daragoj stock from Finland.

Arg. Ch. Blackspot Up To Date, fifteen-inch bitch (Arg. Ch. Mund Harrowill's Alien ex Arg. Ch. Blackspot Tinkerbell), owned by Ruben and Monica Sosa Quiroga of Argentina.

ARGENTINA

Rio de Janeiro is the locus of the Endless Summer Kennel of Maria Fernanda Faria Macedo, who based her line on other kennels' imports from Rossut (United Kingdom) and Johjean (United States), as well as Brazilian Dreamland and Bangor stock. The first show Beagle, Eng. Ch. Barvae Kucky, came to Argentina in 1959, followed by another import, Eng. Ch. Barvae Damper, in 1961. The owner, Mrs. Hilda Rumboll, bred the first Beagle to take a Best in Show at an all-breed event in Argentina.

The kennel that has had the greatest impact on Argentinian Beagles is Mr. and Mrs. Marcos Adler's Pumar, the line based on Rossut (United Kingdom) breeding. Pumar breeding has also played a part in Brazilian Beagledom, as has already been noted in the discussion of Brazilian Beagles. A leading Beagle breeder in the 1980s and 1990s has been Monica Sosa Quiroga (Blackspot Kennel) of Buenos Aires, who has combined multiple bloodlines from the United Kingdom (Rossut and Dufosee), the United States (The Whim's through Brazilian get, Pixshire, Fircone and Starbuck), as well as Finland (Daragoj), also via Brazilian breeders.

Field Trial Events are not held in Argentina, and the popularity of the Beagle as a pet is increasing.

COLOMBIA

Colombia is a relative newcomer on the Beagle scene with only a limited number of Beaglers. Ruby Perdomo (Sarabanda), Cali, is a young enthusiastic breeder/exhibitor who has combined American bloodlines (Sure Luv and The Whim's and, more recently, Dreams Of) in her show stock with considerable success. Another breeder, German Garcia (Gegar Kennels), has also based his line on the wise use of American imports.

chapter 2

The Beagle Standard

The importance of a breed Standard was clearly expressed in the Remarks section that prefaced the American Beagle Club Standard drafted in January 1884, which—with the establishment of the American Kennel Club later that year—became the first official AKC Standard for the breed.

REMARKS

Beagle breeders are aware of the fact that a Standard and Scale of Points are an absolute necessity, so that an authorized type of the Beagle Hound is made apparent for Bench Show judges to base their decisions on, as no two are similar in opinion as to merit, and their ideas differ widely in their estimates as to quality and the breed marks of the race.

Avoiding the recognition of harrier-sized dogs at one show and favoring the smallest specimens at another is one of the objects of the compilers of the Standard and Scale of Points of the American Beagle Club. The judge can use an accepted Standard as a guide to lead him through the difficulties of his position. Breeders and novices can use the Standard to discard those animals deficient in quality and recognize merit where it exists, thus elevating the status of the kennel.

Compiled by Gen. Richard Rowett, Dr. H.L. Twaddell and Norman Elmore, this first Standard was based on and differed little from the English Standard for the Beagle or from the English Foxhound Standard. In fact, as will be seen in the pages that follow, the Standard has changed little to this day. The 1884 Standard attributed 35 points for the head, as opposed to 25 points in the current Standard. It also listed "a thinly haired rattish tail" and "a short, close and nappy coat" as disqualifications, whereas the current Standard lists them, in slightly different language, as defects. In respect to terminology, it is interesting that the 1884 Standard had this appendage:

> Note: Dogs possessing such serious faults as are enumerated under the heading of "Disqualifications" are under the grave suspicion of being of *impure* blood.
>
> Under the heading of "Defects" objectionable features are indicated, such departures from the Standard not however impugning the purity of the breeding.

STANDARD AND SCALE OF POINTS FOR THE BEAGLE HOUND

Adopted by the American Beagle Club—Drafted in January 1884

HEAD

The skull should be moderately domed at the occiput, with the cranium broad and full. The ears set on low, long and fine in texture, the forward or front edge closely framing and inturned to the cheek, rather broad and rounded at the tips, with an almost entire absence of erectile power at their origin.

The eyes full and prominent, rather wide apart, soft and lustrous, and brown or hazel in color. The orbital processes well developed. The expression gentle, subdued and pleading.

The muzzle of medium length, squarely cut, the stop well defined. The jaws should be level. Lips either free from or with moderate flews. Nostrils large, moist and open.

DEFECTS.   A flat skull narrow across the top of the head, absence of dome. Ears short, set on too high, or when the dog is excited rising above the line of the skull at their points of origin due to an excess of erectile power. Ears pointed at the tips, thick or boardy in substance or carried out from the cheek showing a space between. Eyes of light or yellow color. Muzzle long and snipey. Pig jaws or the reverse known as undershot. Lips showing deep *pendulous* flews.

DISQUALIFICATIONS.   Eyes close together, small, beady and terrier-like.

NECK AND THROAT

Neck rising free and light from the shoulders, strong in substance, yet not loaded, of medium length. The throat clean and free from folds of skin, a slight wrinkle below the angle of the jaw however may be allowable.

DEFECTS.   A thick, short, cloddy neck, carried on a line with the top of the shoulder. Throat showing dewlap and folds of skin to a degree termed "throatiness."

SHOULDERS AND CHEST

Shoulders somewhat declining, muscular, but not loaded, conveying the idea of freedom of action, with lightness, activity and strength. Chest moderately broad and full.

DEFECTS. Upright shoulders and a disproportionately wide chest.

BACK, LOIN AND RIBS

Back short, muscular and strong. Loin broad and slightly arched, and the ribs well sprung, giving abundant lung room.

DEFECTS. A long or swayed back, a flat narrow loin, or a flat constricted rib.

FORELEGS AND FEET

Forelegs straight with plenty of bone. Feet close, firm, and either round or harelike in form.

DEFECTS. Out elbows. Knees knuckled over or forward, or bent backward. Feet open and spreading.

HIPS, THIGHS, HIND LEGS AND FEET

Hips strongly muscled, giving abundant propelling power. Stifles strong and well let down. Hocks firm, symmetrical and moderately bent. Feet close and firm.

DEFECTS. Cow hocks and open feet.

TAIL

The tail should be carried gaily, well up and with medium curve, rather short as compared with size of the dog, and clothed with a decided brush.

DEFECTS. A long tail, with a teapot curve.

DISQUALIFICATIONS. *A thinly haired rattish tail, with entire absence of brush.*

COAT

Moderately coarse in texture, and of good length.

DISQUALIFICATIONS. A short, close, and nappy coat.

HEIGHT

The meaning of the term "Beagle" (a word of Celtic origin, and in old English *Begele*) is *small, little*. The dog was so named from his diminutive size. Your committee therefore for the sake of consistency, and that the

Beagle shall be in *fact* what his name implies, strongly recommends that the height line be sharply drawn at fifteen inches, and that all dogs exceeding that height shall be disqualified as over-grown, and outside the pale of recognition.

COLOR

All hound colors are admissible. Perhaps the most popular is black, white and tan. Next in order is the lemon and white, then blue and lemon mottles, then follow the solid colors, such as black and tan, tan, lemon, fawn, etc.

This arrangement is of course arbitrary, the question being one governed entirely by fancy. The colors first named form the most lively contrast and blend better in the pack, the solid colors being sombre and monotonous to the eye.

It is not intended to give a point value to color in the scale for judging, as before said all true hound colors being correct. The foregoing remarks on the subject are therefore simply suggestive.

GENERAL APPEARANCE

A miniature fox-hound, solid and big for his inches, with the wear and tear look of the dog that can last in the chase and follow his quarry to the death.

SCALE OF POINTS

HEAD	Points
Skull	5
Ears	15
Eyes	10
Muzzle, Jaws & Lips	5
BODY	Points
Neck	5
Shoulders & Chest	10

Back & Loins	15
Ribs	5
RUNNING GEAR	Points
Forelegs & Feet	10
Hips, Thighs & Hindlegs	10
COAT & STERN	Points
Tail	5
Coat	5
TOTAL POINTS	100

AKC STANDARD FOR THE ENGLISH FOXHOUND
(For Reference and Comparison)

HEAD   Should be of full size, but by no means heavy. Brow pronounced, but not high or sharp. There should be a good length and breadth, sufficient to give in a dog hound a girth in front of the ears of fully 16 inches. The nose should be long (4 1/2 inches) and wide, with open nostrils. Ears set low and lying close to the cheeks. Most English hounds are "rounded," which means that about 1 1/2 inches is taken off the end of the ear. The teeth must meet squarely, either a *pig mouth* (overshot) or undershot being a disqualification.

NECK   Must be long and clean, without the slightest throatiness, not less than 10 inches from cranium to shoulder. It should taper nicely from shoulders to head, and the upper outline should be slightly convex.

SHOULDERS   Should be long and well clothed with muscle, without being heavy, especially at the points. They must be well sloped, and the true arm between the front and the elbow must be long and muscular, but free from fat or lumber.

CHEST AND BACK RIBS   The chest should girth over 31 inches in a 24-inch hound, and the back ribs must be very deep.

BACK AND LOIN   Must both be very muscular, running into each other without any contraction between them. The couples must be wide, even to raggedness, and the topline of the back should be absolutely level, the

Stern well set on and carried gaily but not in any case curved *over* the back like a squirrel's tail. The ends should taper to a point, and there should be a fringe of hair below. The **Hindquarters** or propellers are required to be very strong, and as endurance is of even greater consequence than speed, straight stifles are preferred to those much bent, as in a Greyhound. **Elbows** set quite straight, and neither turned in nor out are a *sine qua non*. They must be well let down by means of the long true arm above mentioned.

LEGS AND FEET   Every Master of Foxhounds insists on legs as straight as a post, and as strong; size of bone at the ankle being especially regarded as all important. The desire for straightness had a tendency to produce knuckling-over, which at one time was countenanced, but in recent years this defect has been eradicated by careful breeding and intelligent adjudication, and one sees very little of this trouble in the best modern Foxhounds. The bone cannot be too large, and the feet in all cases should be round and catlike, with well-developed knuckles and strong horn, which last is of greatest importance.

COLOR AND COAT   Not regarded as very important, so long as the former is a good "hound color," and the latter is short, dense, hard and glossy. Hound colors are black, tan and white, or any combination of these three, also the various "pies" compounded of white and the color of the hare and badger, or yellow or tan. The **Symmetry** of the Foxhound is of the greatest importance, and what is known as "quality" is highly regarded by all good judges.

SCALE OF POINTS

Head	5
Neck	10
Shoulders	10
Chest and Back Ribs	10
Back and Loin	15
Hindquarters	10
Elbows	5
Legs and Feet	20

Color and Coat	5
Stern	5
Symmetry	5
TOTAL	100

DISQUALIFICATION

Pig-Mouth (overshot) or undershot.
   Approved 1935

ENGLISH BEAGLE STANDARD
(Revised, 1988)

Note: All changes from the previous standard are italicized.

General Appearance   A sturdy, compactly-built hound, conveying the impression of quality without coarseness.

Characteristics   A merry hound whose essential function is to hunt, primarily hare, by following a scent. Bold, with great activity, stamina and determination. Alert, intelligent, and of even temperament.

Temperament [new clause]   Amiable and alert, showing no aggression or timidity.

Head and Skull   Fair length, *powerful without being coarse*, finer in the bitch, *free from frown or wrinkle*. Skull slightly domed, moderately wide, with *slight* peak. Stop well defined and dividing length, between occiput and tip of nose, as equally as possible. Muzzle not snipey, lips reasonably well flewed.

Nose   Broad, preferably black, but less pigmentation permissible in the lighter colored hounds. *Nostrils wide.*

Eyes   Dark brown or hazel, fairly large, not deepset or *prominent*, set well apart with mild appealing expression.

Ears   Long, with *rounded* tip, reaching nearly to end of nose when drawn out. Set on low, fine in texture and hanging gracefully close to *cheeks*.

Mouth   *The jaws should be strong, with perfect, regular and complete scissor bite, i.e., the upper teeth closely overlapping the lower teeth, and set square to the jaw.*

Neck Sufficiently long to enable the hound to come down to scent easily, slightly arched and *showing little* dewlap.

Forequarters *Shoulders well laid back, not loaded.* Forelegs straight and upright, well under the hound, good substance, and round in the bone, not tapering off to feet. Pasterns short. Elbows firm, turning neither in nor out. Height to elbow about half height at withers.

Body Topline straight and level. *Chest let down* to below *elbow.* Ribs well sprung and extending well back. Short *in the* couplings *but well balanced.* Loins powerful and supple, without excessive tuck-up.

Hindquarters *Muscular thighs.* Stifles well bent. Hocks firm, well let down and parallel to each other.

Feet Tight and firm. Well knuckled up and strongly padded. Not harefooted. Nails short.

Tail Sturdy, *moderately long.* Set on high, carried gaily but not curled over back or inclined forward from the root. Well covered with hair, especially on underside.

Gait/Movement Back level, *firm with no indication of roll.* Stride free, long reaching *in front* and straight without high action. Hind legs showing drive. Should not move close behind or paddle or plait in front.

Coat Short, dense and weatherproof.

Color Any recognized hound color other than liver. Tip of stern white.

Size Desirable minimum height at withers 33 cm (13 in.). Desirable maximum height at withers 40 cm (16 in.).

Faults [new clause] Any departure from the foregoing points should be considered a fault, and the seriousness with which the fault should be regarded should be in exact proportion to its degree.

Note [new clause] Male animals should have two apparently normal testicles fully descended into the scrotum.

VISUALIZATION OF THE CURRENT OFFICIAL AKC STANDARD FOR THE BEAGLE

(Approved September 10, 1957)
Illustrated by Pamela Powers-Zelenz

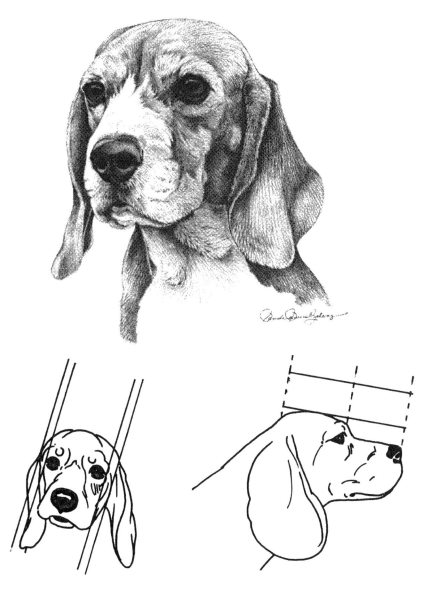

Correct head—Planes of skull and muzzle should be parallel. Length of skull from occiput to stop should be approximately equal to length of muzzle from stop to tip of nose. Ears should be set on level with outer corner of eye.

Incorrect—Skull too wide and flat, eyes small with harsh expression.

Incorrect—Muzzle snipy, ears short and high-set.

Incorrect—Skull domey, stop exaggerated.

Incorrect—Flat skull, small eye, lacking in lip.

Incorrect—Bulging prominent eye, short muzzle.

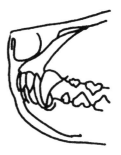

Correct Scissors Bite—Level bite permissible.

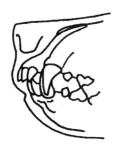

Incorrect—Overshot bite.

Incorrect—Undershot bite.

Correct—Length and thickness of neck. Note arch of neck below occiput.

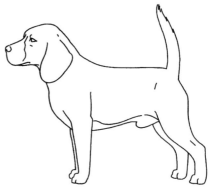

Incorrect—Short, thick neck.

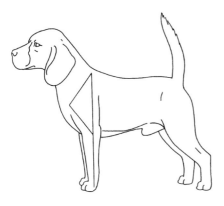

Correct—Shoulder assembly and placement of foreleg in relation to shoulder. Note depth of chest to elbow and amount of forechest visible.

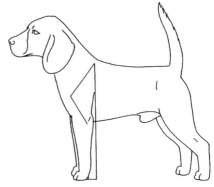

Incorrect—Placement of upper arm (humerus). Note shallow forechest.

Correct—Clean shoulder.

Incorrect—Heavy in shoulder with crooked forelegs.

Correct—Topline.

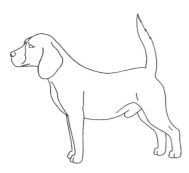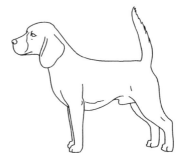

Incorrect—Long back with sagging topline.

Incorrect—Too much tuck-up.

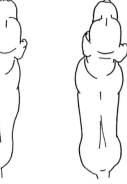

Correct—Rib spring and balance as viewed from above. Note equal width of shoulders, chest and pelvis.

Incorrect—(left) Narrow pelvis in relation to width of shoulder; (right) flat ribs and chest.

Incorrect—(left) Out at elbows, toeing-in; (right) crooked forelegs, heavy in shoulder.

Correct—Clean shoulder, straight forelegs.

Correct—Cat foot.

Incorrect—(left) Hare foot with elongated central two toes; (right) down at pastern.

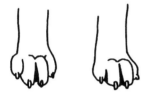

Incorrect—Flat, spread foot.

 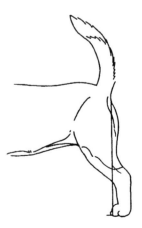

Correct—Rear angulation. Note that perpendicular line drawn from base of tail falls through front of hind foot.

Incorrect—(top left) Excessive angulation. Note that perpendicular line drawn from base of tail to ground falls forward of hind foot; (left) lacking in angulation.

Correct—Placement of hind legs. A perpendicular line dropped from the outer iliac crest should pass through the hock joint and foot.

Incorrect—(left) Cow-hocks; (center) narrow rear; (right) bow legs.

Correct—Tail and tail set.

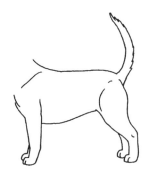

Incorrect—Tail too long
and thin with low tail set.

Incorrect—Gay tail.

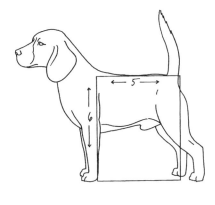

Correct—Balance. Note ratio of length to height (5:6) as measured from tip of withers to base of tail and tip of withers to ground. Distance between withers and ground is equally divided by elbow and depth of chest.

Incorrect—Short on leg with distance between point of elbow and ground **less** than from point of elbow to tip of withers.

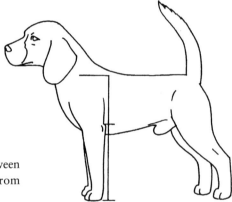

Incorrect—Too high on leg with distance between point of elbow and ground **greater** than from elbow to tip of withers.

Incorrect—Too long.

Correct—Side gait.

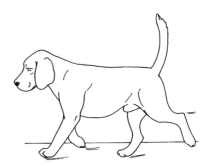

Incorrect—Restricted reach and drive.

Correct—Front movement.

Correct—Rear movement.

Hounds at full cry.

Northern Hare Beagle Club.

Monroe Beagle Club, Monroe, Georgia, Cherokee Trials.

chapter 3

Beagles in the Field

A man, his Beagle, and his gun form a triad that might well have been written into the Constitution of the United States or the Bill of Rights.

For the solitary hunter, it was a natural step to join with others in organized Beagle field activities. The original Pack Trials based on the English tradition, in which hounds hunted in three-, four- and eight-couple packs and judged on the merit of the pack as a whole, were and still are, to some extent, a moneyed sport.

The traditional or formal pack huntsman and his whippers-in or assistants dress in green jackets, white pants, black shoes and black caps. Individual piping on the jackets distinguishes one pack from another. This oldest form of Beagle Trials in the United States still flourishes today, with subscription packs (supported not by the huntsman alone but by interested Beaglers) joining private packs at the Spring and Fall Trials at the National Beagle Club running grounds at Institute Farm, Aldie, Virginia.

In the early 1900s, individual hunters owned at most four Beagles and hunted, not on large estates, but in their rural neighborhoods, which organized Beagle Clubs. Trials were held in which the hounds were judged individually while working in pairs by sex and size, known as "Brace Trials," as well as "Small Pack," usually consisting of four to seven hounds, and "large pack," with as many as thirty to sixty in a class.

The number of Beagle Clubs holding Field Trials mushroomed in the United States and Canada, with the kind of trial run determined by the terrain and available game. The small cottontail rabbit, as well as the sand rabbit of Texas, flourishes in land with brush and cover, runs a small swing and goes to ground readily. The swifter varying or snowshoe hare is much larger, quite intelligent, leaves a stronger scent, runs in wide swings, does not go to ground and thrives in mountainous and swampy terrain.

The Beagle that hunted cottontail and in the trials needed to work only up to forty minutes at a time, was selectively bred over the years for less speed, more meticulous tracking and a very keen sense of smell. The hound run on hare required more speed and greater endurance to run several hours at a time, and less emphasis was placed on keen scenting ability. These Beagles were bred to be larger in size and longer in limb.

The original good Field Trial Beagles performed well on both types of game, but increasing specialization has led to two quite different-looking hounds.

With the loss of undeveloped land to growing cities and suburban sprawl during the twentieth century, the early Field Trial clubs found it necessary to purchase or lease acreage for their functions. It is a requirement of the American Kennel Club that each member or recognized Field Trial club have its own running grounds. Newer clubs lease their land from private coal or paper companies, wildlife preserves or state-owned acreage. Fencing of the property became mandatory to prevent hounds in pursuit of game from crossing heavily-trafficked highways. This, in turn, affected the rabbit's behavior, requiring even more selective breeding for a slower, more methodically-working Beagle.

Serious Beaglers have joined the ranks of conservationists to protect the land needed for wild-game propagation and survival. Some clubs sponsor rabbit- and hare-breeding programs in an attempt to replenish the diminishing supply of rabbits and hares.

During 1996, over 500 licensed Beagle Field Events were run in the United States. Of these, approximately 350 were Brace Trials, 160 Small Pack Option (SPO), and 40 Large Pack. In addition, 100 Field Trial clubs exist that do not have annual trials but whose members run their Beagles in other clubs' trial events.

ORGANIZATION

The Beagle Advisory Committee (BAC), composed of twelve members and chaired by a member of the American Kennel Club executive staff, oversees the licensing of Beagle Field Trials. In 1936, the National Beagle Club, inundated by the growing number of Field Trials, surrendered its responsibility as a parent club in this sphere of activity to the BAC. The American Kennel Club appoints members to the committee from delegates representing AKC member clubs. The BAC has proven to be an administrative body responsive to the changing needs of Field Trial Beaglers.

Yellow Creek Ben, a product of the famous Yellow Creek Kennels. *The Beagle Yearbook*, 1945

Fd. Ch. Sammy R, an outstanding hunter and sire during the 1940s, sired by Fd. Ch. Yellow Creek Sport, an impressive stud during the late 1930s. Sammy was owned by Ike and Anna Carril, original owners/ publishers of *Hounds & Hunting*. *Hounds & Hunting*

BEAGLE REGISTRIES

In addition to the American Kennel Club (AKC), the United Kennel Club (UKC) and the American Rabbit Hunters Association (ARHA) offer registration for the Field Beagle. All three organizations sponsor trials. The UKC sponsors conformation competition as well.

AKC FIELD TRIALS

There are three primary kinds of Beagle Field Trials: those held by AKC member clubs, those held by nonmember clubs licensed to hold Field Trials, and Field Trials sanctioned by the American Kennel Club and held by both member and nonmember clubs. Championship points are awarded to winners of only the first two Field Trials.

Each club is limited to one field event per year. In recent years, another kind of trial has emerged: the Dissimilar Trials. Where Brace and SPO clubs have merged, two kinds of trials are allowed per year: one Brace and the other either SPO or Large Pack.

MEASUREMENT

Basically, a Beagle must be officially eligible for its class by size. Rules for the timing of measurement and by whom vary with the kind of trial, whether Brace, Small Pack, Large Pack or Small Pack Option. Official measurement cards attesting to under thirteen-inch and between thirteen-inch and fifteen-inch are also available under American Kennel Club regulations.

Large Pack Trials require measurement in the morning prior to running. Brace, Small Pack and Small Pack Option Trials permit premeasurement (prior to judging) if requested. Ordinarily, measurement is done on the six to ten Beagles called back by the judge after the first series that are eligible for the second series.

JUDGING

Two judges are required for Brace, Small Pack and Large Pack Field Trials. Additional judges may be needed for Large Pack Trials if the number of entries is large.

As the *Beagle Field Trial Rules* state, "The Beagle is a trailing hound whose purpose is to find game, to pursue it in an energetic and decisive manner and to show determination to account for it."

Points on which judges base their decisions are searching ability, pursuing ability, accuracy, proper use of voice, endurance, competitive spirit (only a plus when focused on running game, not beating other hounds) and intelligence.

Fd. Ch. Walk-A-Line Roxie (Fd. Ch. River Rock Rocky ex Fd. Ch. Walk-A-Line Brenda), winner of the 1996 Purina Outstanding Field Trial Beagle award. According to owner, Mike Mock, she "makes a good effort on every rabbit she's put on and is just a real brainy Beagle." *Hounds & Hunting*

Placings first to fourth, as well as fifth place Next Best Qualified (NBQ), are awarded in each class. Judging is a process of elimination, with the winners of each class competing in a second series and ultimately a Winners Pack from which the winner in that variety is selected.

BRACE BEAGLES

Called Walkie-Talkie, the Brace Beagle needs to do only that: walk and talk. Over the years, faster Beagles that consistently overran the rabbit's trail and failed to "check" (turn back immediately to find where the rabbit turned) were eliminated from the breeding pool. This resulted in slower, more precise workers. Since many Brace Beaglers are older, the slower pace enables them to keep up comfortably with their hounds. Newer and younger Beaglers seem to prefer a more active hound and are gravitating toward the SPO Beagle.

Brace clubs are organized into seven regional federations. Each hosts an annual trial, spaced throughout the late winter and spring months. The winners of the seven Futurity and seven Derby Events complete in a final event, the winner of which is awarded the Purina Top Field Dog prize. In 1996, Fd. Ch. Walk-A-Line Roxie, owned by Mike Mock, captured the Purina Outstanding Field Trial Beagle award. Roxie made history with this win; for the first time in twenty-four years, the winner was owner-bred, started, finished and handled.

Training of young Beagles begins when they reach six or seven months of age. The pups are placed in a starting pen of at least one acre of enclosed hunting area stocked with rabbits, where they learn to use their noses and get the feel of hunting. At about fourteen to sixteen months, the young Beagles are run individually or in a brace for another six months of training. Bringing the young Beagle along slowly gives the "gunner" the opportunity to select his best hounds for the first Field Trial.

Parade of thirteen-inch Champions, 1996 Deep South Federation. *Hounds & Hunting*

Winners—fifteen-inch Derby bitches, Heartland Federation, 1996. *Hounds & Hunting*

Winners—fifteen-inch Open Dog Class Conformation Show, 1994 Pennsylvania Beagle Gundog Association. The winner was SPO Fd. Ch. Misty Mountain Bugler (extreme left), bred, owned and handled by Stan Hepler. Bugler was the Grand Final Winner with first place in both Field Trial and Conformation Show at the 1995 PBGA Championship. *Kristine Kraeuter*

The thirteen-inch Futurity bitches, second series, Southern Federation. *Hounds & Hunting*

SMALL PACK OPTION BEAGLES

By the 1970s, concern was growing among a large group of rabbit hunters that the Brace Beagle was losing its ability to run and hunt. As a result, what is known as the "gundog movement" grew quickly, leading the American Kennel Club in 1977 to license testing for gunshyness in what is known as the Small Pack Option. This system selects the best hounds of a first series of four to seven Beagles to run in a second series, the winners of which compete in the Winners Pack. During the course of the trial, a shot, using a blank cartridge from a 20-gauge shotgun or a .32 or large pistol, is fired after all the Beagles are working a trail.

The gundog movement now has clubs in twelve states, each with forty to fifty members. The clubs, in turn, have formed regional federations.

A significant step taken by the United Beagle Gundog Federation is the requirement, as of 1987, that any Beagle competing in a qualifying trial and the National Run-off must be a dual entry in both field and conformation. Grand Final Winner and Grand Final Runner-up awards are presented to those Beagles with the highest and second-highest number of points accumulated in field and conformation judging. Other gundog federations are adopting this option as well. This represents the first organized push toward reestablishing the ideal of a proper-looking working Beagle. Some federations have organized educational programs to teach both judges and Field Beaglers what constitutes good conformation.

Training of a gundog, which must not only hunt but not shy from a gunshot, begins with an introduction to loud noises at an early age. Some Beaglers accompany feeding times with loud, startling sounds by shooting blank cartridges or banging a spoon against a pan. Obedience training also prepares the hound for its first trip into the field at about six months of age. A younger pup learns too easily mistakes that will be difficult to correct.

Int. Fed. Ch. Caravoic's Blue Ninja, fourteen and three-fourths inches (FTC Branko's Jack Of All Trades ex Greenbriar Branko's Tootsie), a product of excellent bloodlines that works with extreme concentration, desire and drive. Owner: Victor V. Costanza. *Better Beagling*

Fd. Ch. Eagles Up Sea Sparrow, thirteen inches (IFC Round Pound M.T. ex Sunapee Mt. Big Bertha), owned by David A. Smith, is typical of the Hare Hounds currently being run.

The fifteen-inch Bitch class, Kuyahoora Hare Trials, New York, 1996. *Better Beagling*

Training takes place in 10-, 40-, and 100-acre enclosures. The pups start working with the older, experienced pack. Once they have learned the rules, they are then worked with younger, more aggressive Beagles. After three months, both owner and trainer evaluate the Beagles. At eight months, it is possible to select the best and place the others as individual hunting dogs.

With the growing emphasis on good-looking hounds, show training is also a part of the Beagle gundog's early training, starting at five or six weeks.

LARGE PACK ON HARE

No doubt the most exciting form of field work is done by a pack of thirty to sixty Beagles running joyously in pursuit of the large hare. These hounds run so swiftly that even a man on horseback cannot keep up. Hare hunting runs in the blood of its enthusiasts.

The Northern Hare Beagle Club of New York, established in 1916, was the first to concentrate on holding pack stakes on the snowshoe hare and the first to hold a licensed hare stake.

Today, active clubs exist in all the hare states. The ten hare clubs of Northern Michigan and the lower Michigan peninsula comprise the Northern Michigan Hare Association. This group, plus the Hare Association of the Eastern United States, which includes Maine, Vermont, New Hampshire, New York and Massachusetts, are overseen by the Federation of Large Pack on Hare.

Circuits, a series of trials given by regional clubs at the best time of year for hunting, attract many participants.

Early bloodlines included L.M. Watson's Yellow Creek line in Missouri and Harvey Low's Shady Lake Beagles in New York, two of the best-producing kennels during the 1920s and 1930s. Mr. Low's Fd. Ch. Flip of Shady Lake, a product of two Conformation Champions, exemplified the dual use of the Beagle of that day. Fd. Ch. Sammy R, out of Yellow Creek stock, was an outstanding producer of both field and Conformation Champions. Sammy R was owned by Ike and Anna Carrel, the original owners and publishers of the magazine *Hounds & Hunting*. A grandson of Sammy R's, Fd. Ch. Gray's Linesman, sired fifty field champions in the 1950s.

Both Yellow Creek and Shady Lake were tightly inbred lines. Harvey Low, with his excellent sense of good quality, introduced new blood occasionally and always with good results. His theory was, "You don't need a special hound for hare trials, just a good hound."

At the time of Sammy R, who completed his championship in 1938, it was not unusual for a good hound to win at both Rabbit and Hare Trials.

In recent history, IFC Able's East Coast Trimmer, dog, and IFC Birch Haven Bruiser, dog, are two of the best-known hare hounds. FC Dingus MacRae, with an excellent reputation in Large Pack, has sired progeny that have done well in SPO. As Pearl Baker, Editor of *Better Beagling*, states, "There just is not as much difference between a good 'harehound' and a good 'cottontail hound' as many people insist in believing!"

Puppy training starts early on the cottontail rabbit. Once the puppies learn line control, the ability to follow the rabbit's trail, training on hares begins. Enclosures are not used, because the hare could be easily caught. A promising hare hunter will be obvious by its first birthday with performance peaking at four or five years of age. Because such physical stamina is required of the hounds, the older Beagles simply cannot perform as well.

Run very differently from other kinds of Field Trials, Hare Trials require the Beagles to run for at least eight hours. The judges, spotted about the terrain, allow the dogs two hours of running time to find the hare's trail before they begin judging. Throughout the day at regular intervals, two or more judges meet to compare notes and to eliminate some Beagles from further consideration at each conference. However, all the hounds continue to run until they tire or the trial is over and the winners are selected.

"On Line," Large Pack, International Beagle Hare Futurity, 1994, Vermont Beagle Club, Hardwick, Vermont. *Better Beagling*

chapter 4

Starting and Training a Pack of Beagles

by David B. Sharp, Jr.

(Joint Master of the Nantucket-Treweryn Beagles)

Note: This chapter has been reprinted from *Hounds & Hunting,* November & December, 1983.

David (Bun) Sharp's Treweryn Pack was formed in 1924. He was widely recognized, in both the United States and England, as an expert huntsman. His Field Ch. Treweryn's Forger, which Bun described as "terrible looking but with a phenomenal nose," won the three-hour stakes in 1931, a win he repeated for three consecutive years. Treweryn's Bugle, a thirteen-inch male, was his most important stud. Sire of ten to twelve litters, when bred to Nantucket's Hoodwink, he produced Beagles of great hunting ability and good Beagle type.

Becky Sharp, Bun's wife and Joint Master of the Nantucket-Treweryn Pack, began her pack experience in Nantucket, whipping in with some of the finest huntsmen and packs of the day. In 1925, she founded the Nantucket Pack, using as her foundation bitches two English imports, O'Berkeley Primula and Bolebroke Heiress. After their marriage, Bun and Becky competed with their packs but then merged them in 1964 to form the remarkable Nantucket-Treweryn pack.

Becky and Bun died in 1988 within six months of each other, both in their eighties. Nantucket-Treweryn continues on today as a subscription pack.

J.M.

The Merry Beaglers.

Treweryn Beagles, David B. Sharp, Master. Oil painting by W. West Frazier IV. *Nancy Stettinius*

I originally wrote most of this article over forty years ago for *Hounds &*
Hunting and will now try to bring it up to 1983.

At the request of the editor, I am writing my thoughts on the organizing,
training and management of a pack of Beagles. These suggestions are by no
means to be considered a commentary on the sport of Beagling, but are merely
my conclusions based on our experience over the last fifty-four years, and
are given with the hope of being useful to anyone intending to start a pack.
Several interesting and thoroughly exhaustive books have been published on
this sport, of which a few are *The Art of Beagling*, by J. Otho Paget; *Hare*
Hunting and Harriers, by H.A. Bryden and *Hints on Beagling*, by Peter Wood.
I cannot recommend these books too strongly, and of the three, I consider
The Art of Beagling to be the best.

Beagling, or the sport of hunting the hare with packs of small hounds or
Beagles, is indeed an ancient sport predating that of foxhunting. Suffice it to
say here that Nimrod, who lived 2,000 years before the birth of Christ, is
credited with having hunted the hare, and Xenophon, who lived 350 years
B.C., was definitely known to be an enthusiastic and regular hare hunter.

There are today in England eighty-four packs of foot harriers and Beagles
as against sixty-eight in 1938. In the United States, there are now twenty-
nine active packs of Beagles with collars registered with the National Beagle
Club of America against twenty packs in 1938. Thus, we can safely say that
the sport as practiced by packs is showing a healthy growth in popularity, to
say nothing of the terrific increase in the number of Field Trials held in this
country for single hounds and the number of hounds competing in these trials and Bench Shows. However, twenty-nine active registered packs is still a
very small number for America when compared with eighty-four in England.
The reason is, in part, that there are probably hundreds of sportsmen in this
country who own and regularly hunt a pack of six or eight couples of Beagles
without an organization or the formality of green coats with collars registered with the National Beagle Club. This article is dedicated to those who
would like to perpetuate the sport in the traditional English manner as is now
being done by the active registered packs in this country.

THE COUNTRY

The first point to be considered by anyone wishing to start a pack of Beagles
is, "Where will we hunt?" The type of country to be selected depends largely
on the quarry to be hunted. Most sections of the United States abound with
cottontail rabbits, and if this is the quarry to be hunted, almost any type of
country will do unless it is so thickly wooded, grown up with undergrowth
and filled with such deep swamps that it would be impossible to stay with
your hounds when running or see much of their work. The ideal cottontail
country to my mind would contain sufficient woods, clumps of undergrowth
and briar patches to harbor game in bad weather and protect it from vermin,

and at the same time have open fields between coverts so that the rabbits when driven would leave covert and circle or, if driven hard, would run straight away into the open to the next patch. Whether your quarry be hare or rabbit, pastureland is the best as scent always seems to lie better on grass than on plowed or barren land.

If hares, either European or Kansas Jacks, are to be hunted, a more open type of country should be selected. The more grass or pastureland the better, gently rolling but not too hilly. A hill may often be a fine place from which to view a hunt, but if it is too steep and your pack drives a hare straight away over several crests, you will soon wish for a new pair of legs. Always try to pick a country with as few paved roads as possible. I know of no more heartbreaking sight than to see your pack running straight toward a highway crowded with automobiles traveling at fifty-five miles an hour and not be able to get to your hounds to stop them or to get to the road to stop traffic. It is indeed a miracle that more hounds are not killed by autos, considering the number of roads crossed in the average run of a hare.

Snowshoe or varying hares and swamp rabbits may also be hunted in certain sections of the country, but the natural habitat of these animals does not lend itself to following your hounds closely on foot or seeing much of their work. Many excellent runs may be had on the Northern hare, but not to the satisfaction of those who like to run with their hounds and watch them work closely.

After selecting your country, the next step is to make friends with the farmers and other landowners and get permission to hunt over their land. Never forget that the farmer is and must be your best friend. Without his friendship, none of us could get far with our sport, and there is no more annoying experience than to have a hare shot ahead of your hounds or to be loudly told to "get the hell off my place!" It is not enough to merely get permission to hunt over a farm. Always stop to see the owner or tenant before you start your day's hunt, or if you run onto his land from that of a neighbor, do not fail to call a greeting as you pass. If you send out a notice of the time and place of the hunts for the month, as is customary with most packs, be sure that you send one to those whose land you propose to cross, and always invite them to hunt with you. You will soon find that the farmers will take a keen interest in the sport, often driving miles and bringing their whole family to see the chase. They are invaluable for protecting hares during the gunning season, and I have known farmers who have issued orders that no hares are to be shot on their property, as they prefer to see the "Bagles" run them.

An annual puppy show held at your kennels is a most enjoyable event to which all landowners should be asked to come. If you can get your farmers to raise some puppies for you and bring them to the show next year, you will have accomplished a great good for the sport and your pack, as farm-raised hounds are far superior to those raised in a kennel. This is called putting puppies out "at walk" and should build up much interest in your pack. While on the subject of the country, it should be mentioned that great care should be exercised not to do damage to crops, fences, etc when running. A field of 100–150 people, a frequent occurrence with many of our large packs in the East, may do considerable damage if wheat or new grass is run over when the going is soft. A broken fence or a gate thoughtlessly left open may cause livestock to get out and do terrific damage, to say nothing of the time lost by the farmer in recapturing them. Finally, do not pick a country that is already being hunted by an established pack of Beagles or Foxhounds unless you have their permission and the country is big enough for all.

PROBABLE EXPENSES

Having located a suitable country and learned what is necessary to keep it open to hunting, the matter of expenses should be taken up. To properly maintain a pack of Beagles with all the attendant expenses, such as a kennelman, a hound van, kennels, feed, insurance, veterinary services and license fee will cost anywhere from $2,500 to $5,000 a year.[1] Few men young enough to run after Beagles or hares are so wealthy. It is then necessary to raise the money by forming a club or taking annual subscriptions to meet expenses from those who hunt with the pack. This is a very fair way of sharing expenses, and several of the larger packs in the East are now operated on this basis, having over 100 subscribers.

If the kennel work is done by you or your family and/or with the help of your amateur hunt staff, this expense can be cut in half or more. To save the cost of a hound van, many packs now use a small trailer.

ACQUIRING A PACK

Here the inevitable argument as to thirteen-inch or fifteen-inch hounds is bound to begin and may be carried on far into the night whenever Beaglers meet. To my mind, it is just as silly to argue for or against thirteen-inch or fifteen-inch Beagles as it is to perpetuate the age-old argument of the quality of English Foxhounds versus American Foxhounds. Both types of Foxhounds have their good points, and each is suited to a particular type of country. And so with the two conventional American sizes of Beagles. Pick hounds to suit your country. Fifteen-inch hounds, being naturally faster, will probably kill

---

[1] *Author's note: The above estimate of annual expense was written years ago. Thanks to inflation, it now could be doubled or tripled, depending on whether a full-time kennelman is employed and the size of the kennel. Fifteen couples of hounds are not necessary for cottontail rabbit hunting; in fact, the National Beagle Club will register a pack of four couples and officially list a pack of five couples as a Recognized Pack.*

"Blessing of the Hounds," Opening Day Hunt, Holly Hill Pack, 1994.
Wanda and John Borsa, Joint Masters. *Kristine Kraeuter*

more hares in rough country containing much plowed ground, cornfields and
fields overgrown with weeds than thirteen-inch hounds. It is by far easier for
the big fellows to get over rough ground. However, if your country is very
hilly or you and your staff are not good cross-country runners, better stick to
the small hounds or hunt rabbits, not hares. It is indeed poor sport to see
your pack disappear over a hilltop and, gasping for breath, struggle on in
their wake, never seeing anything of their work until they come to a check.
On a good scenting day, even thirteen-inch hounds will run away from their
field, but generally a fair runner in good condition can keep them in sight. I
personally am an advocate of the thirteen-inch Beagle for either hare or cottontail hunting. However, small hounds have one distinct disadvantage in
that it is a great deal more difficult to obtain good looks in thirteen-inch
hounds than it is in fifteen-inch hounds. If the look of a pack is to be a
primary consideration, then select the fifteen-inch variety.

The huntsman casts the hounds to search for quarry in some promising cover. *Kristine Kraeuter*

The delight in Beagling to a true hound lover is to watch hounds work, and to stay long with Beagling, one must be a hound lover; therefore, pick the size of hound to suit your legs and your country. A good plan would be to hunt with several packs both thirteen-inch and fifteen-inch the season before you start your own pack and compare results over country as similar as possible to the one in which you plan to hunt. This will also enable you to learn how a pack should be handled in the field and to pick out hounds that are good in their work with an idea of buying them after the end of the season. Almost any large pack will sell draft of old hounds after the season to make room for their incoming young entry. When buying hounds to start a pack, it is by far better to purchase four or five couples from one pack that are broken and used to hunting together than to pick an individual here and there and attempt to combine them into a pack.

Starting with a nucleus of, say, four couples of old, steady hounds from two different packs, the balance of the pack can be made of young hounds purchased here and there who will quickly learn what it is all about from the old-timers. Buying hounds in the spring has the double advantage of a cheaper price from the packs who want to lighten up and providing time for pack breaking and road work before the start of the hunting season in the fall.

Concentrate on pack hounds that have been bred by a good, recognized pack for many generations or their bloodlines. Stay away from AKC show hounds or Brace Field Trial hounds. Get as much bloodline going back to the English packs as you can. Their hunting is so much better than anything in this country that there is no comparison. Over there, hounds usually meet at noon and hunt hares until dark, covering miles and miles of country. They can't afford to keep a poor hound, so these are quickly eliminated. All our hounds trace to two bitches that Phil Burrows of the Bolebroke gave us years ago, and we are going to stick to his line.

KENNELMAN AND KENNELS

Before acquiring a pack, it is of course necessary to find someone to take care of them. Most Masters of Beagles carry the horn themselves and are assisted in the field by friends who act as nonpaid honorary whippers-in. The hunt staff, or those handling hounds in the field, should be good runners if hares are to be hunted. There are, however, many more important qualifications for the kennelman than being fleet of foot. First of these should be a love for hounds. An even temper, a quiet voice, cleanliness, patience and willingness to work without regard to hours are all equally important attributes of a good kennelman. Beagles are naturally rather mild creatures and will easily become shy if yelled at and beaten by a bad-tempered kennelman or one who is afraid of them. A man who has had experience with Foxhounds or another Beagle kennel and who is too old to act as huntsman should make an excellent kennelman if he has the aforesaid qualifications. This type of man would be particularly desirable if the Master himself is a beginner. If a man with experience cannot be found, then pick a boy or girl who is keen about hounds and hunting and has these qualifications of character. Take him to a good kennel and let him spend a few days watching how others do things. Then talk over the matter of how best to care for your own hounds and set down rules for cleaning kennels, feeding, etc. Everything should be done on a schedule with a fixed time each day for each task. An intelligent person will soon work out his own system based on his equipment and kennels. Don't employ a "grafter"—it often has been said that some stablemen and kennelmen set by a tidy sum from what they get from feed and supply stores. Your kennelman should be thoroughly honest and should be interested in seeing the pack grow and improve. Even so, the Master should arrange all purchases and take away this temptation from his kennelman.

Many of the finest packs of Beagles in America are kenneled in adapted barns or chicken houses. I do not mean to say that this is ideal, but often it is perfectly possible to remodel or adapt an old building to a practical kennel at a great savings in cost. The main things to remember when building a kennel are that it should be on high ground, well lighted and ventilated and warm and dry. The kennel should face south and have lodging rooms for dogs and bitches, separated by an alleyway or entry where hounds can be drawn out and fed. This will also enable visitors to see hounds in bad weather without discomfort to man or beast and provide an excellent place for brushing, doctoring and otherwise working on the hounds under cover. The lodging room should provide wooden benches raised above a cement floor for sleeping

The Holly Hill Pack at full cry. In organized pack hunting, ideally the hounds should be so well matched that when running a "blanket could cover the entire pack." *Kristine Kraeuter*

Huntsman Wanda Borsa prepares to use her horn to call in the hounds at the end of the chase. *Kristine Kraeuter*

Holly Hill Brandy, fifteen-inch bitch (Fd. Ch. Thorn Gap Jack ex Ch. Blanchard's Bugle Ann), excellent pack hound, winner of the fifteen-inch (combined sexes) Three Hour Stakes classes at NBC, Aldie Fall Pack Trials at Aldie, Virginia. Owners: Wanda and John Borsa, Holly Hill Pack.

quarters. Adjoining this would be an ideal place for a room for puppies, and on the opposite side separated by a wall from the kennel, should be a hospital room that can also be used for bitches while whelping or in season. Many variations of this plan have been used, and these suggestions are given to those who contemplate entirely new construction. Hunting Beagles do not need artificial heat except when down with distemper or other illnesses, and in fact, they are generally hardier and healthier without it. The hospital pen should therefore adjoin the feed room or, if in a separate building, should have its own heating.

All lodging rooms should open onto concrete or gravel runs to which hounds should have access at all times. They will quickly learn to use these runs as toilets, which will greatly facilitate cleaning. These runs need not be large but should connect with large grass runs for daytime use.

BREEDING

This is an all-important aspect. The beginner should refer to some of the books mentioned in the beginning of this article and then seek advice from someone with experience. It has been said that "breeding is, at best, a gamble," which may be true, but if carefully handled, the odds against your success may be greatly reduced. Good plus good will not necessarily produce good. The product largely depends on the ancestors of "good" and "good." Breed

The members of a six-week-old Brushy Run litter meet their first rabbit. All but one of these hounds are now serving as personal gundogs for their owners. *Kristine Kraeuter*

first for hunting ability and second for looks. Select for your best bitches the best sires available, and never breed a hound that has an outstanding fault. A pack that does not keep young blood coming in each year will soon die out.

We practice "line breeding," by which we mean breeding a dog to a bitch that has the greatest number of the *same* hounds in each pedigree that are outstandingly good hounds, both in conformation and hunting ability, *PROVIDED* that there is at least one outcross of a hound with completely different (unrelated) breeding in three generations. If you follow this practice and use the right stock, you should end up with an excellent pack of "look-alikes" that have a stamp of their own and eventually will be known by everyone as *your* pack.

If you are lucky enough to breed the right dog to the right bitch and get a litter that is really good both in looks and work, stay with it and keep breeding that pair as often as you can. Don't change your luck and shop around for a new stud dog. Many people do just this, and I can't understand why. Let me give you an example. My good wife and now Joint Master, when she had her own pack, The Nantucket, bred her good bitch, Hoodwink, to Treweryn Bugler four times. The result was a pack that was first place in the eight couples class at the National Field Trials four times out of five years and second place in the remaining year. They also won the fifteen-pack class repeatedly at the Bryn Mawr Hound Show. They were all brothers and sisters!

We do *not* believe in "inbreeding," that is, sire to daughter, son to mother or brother to sister.

From the puppies, weed out the babblers and those that run mute, and get rid of the skirters and backtrackers. Then when your pack is running, "cut off the head and tail"—cull those that are too fast or too slow for the majority. This sounds like brutal treatment, but it is the only way to build up a good pack. Of course, your discarding cannot all be done in the first year or so, but it must eventually be done in this manner if you are to succeed. It may break your heart to sell a hound that always leads your pack, but the fact that he always leads shows that he is too fast for his fellows, and they are forced to follow him without doing their share of the work. The goal to shoot at is a level hunting pack, evenly sized and beautiful to look at.

Good conformation should be an important consideration in breeding, as a hound with a bad shoulder or bad feet cannot run with the ease of his well-made brother. Pay strict attention to this. Buy a copy of *The Beagle Standard* and study it well, but pay no heed to color or markings. You will find it difficult enough to breed hounds of good conformation and good field ability without breeding for color. True are the words "a good hound cannot be a bad color."

Your bitches should be bred so as to whelp in the early spring. The period of gestation is generally between sixty and sixty-five days. There is no

Glenbarr Wolver Hillary, fifteen-inch bitch (Glenbarr Wolver Hazzard ex Wolver Festive), was the winner of the first annual NBC Triple Challenge in 1996. The Challenge is a three-part event in which hounds compete afield in a Brace Trial, Stakes class and a Conformation Show. Placements are based on points earned in all three phases of the competition. *Kristine Kraeuter*

doctor as good as "Old Sol," and puppies raised without summer sun are seldom as healthy and require twice the care if whelped in winter. Now that heat (infrared) lamps are available, we usually breed in February or March so that when the whelps leave their bed, they can get the full benefits of the spring sun. Be very careful in the use of heat lamps, however. We rig ours with a cord through a pulley so that they can be raised or lowered to a height sufficient to keep the floor of the bed warm, not hot. Each lamp should have a safety chain so that if the cord breaks, it cannot fall in the bed. Several kennels have suffered bad fires from this cause, one losing their entire kennel and most of their hounds when a heat lamp fell in the straw.

The bitches should be specially fed on plenty of meat several weeks before due and should, of course, be separated from the other hounds. When the bitch becomes uneasy or starts to make a nest out of her bed, someone should be in frequent attendance. No solid food should then be given, just a little warm soup. It is always best to let nature have her way first, as the majority of the bitches will have their puppies without assistance. But should she labor unduly long, a competent veterinarian should be called in. A pup too large to pass, dead or that has turned may well be the cause of the death of a good bitch, and someone should look at her at frequent intervals during her labor and until all the puppies are whelped to see that all goes well. Instruments may be purchased for the extraction of dead puppies, but I would suggest that the novice leave this to a veterinarian.

FEEDING

There are many prepared dog foods on the market, and most of them are suitable for feeding to hounds. They require no cooking and need only to have water added and allowed to soak. We purchase meat scraps, mostly bone and fat, from a local slaughterhouse, keep it in a freezer and boil a few handfuls to make a soup to pour over the commercial dog food. In the summer on Nantucket Island, we use fish heads and backbones left after filleting instead of meat scraps. They love it, and it makes their coats shine, but it is quite a job to pick the bones out.

chapter 5

Breeding Obedience Beagles

by Marie Shuart & Rosalind Hall

Marie Shuart, Teloca, Reg, has been breeding Beagles for thirty years. Among her dogs are several National Beagle Club Specialty and Sweepstakes winners. Since the 1960s, she has put more than twenty-five Companion Dog titles on her dogs. She won High in Trial at the 1983 National Beagle Club Specialty, as well as Obedience Beagle of the Year for the same year.

Rosalind Hall, Sirius Beagles, has been training Beagles in Obedience for twenty years. She has put seven CDs, four CDXs and two UDs on her Beagles, as well as Obedience titles on several other breeds. She has also titled dogs in Tracking, Herding and Agility. She has taught obedience classes for the Dog Obedience Club of Hollywood, Florida for over fifteen years. Her dogs were Obedience Beagles of the Year for 1987–89, as well as #1 Hound on the Shuman System for 1987–88.

When planning a breeding for Obedience prospects, we would consider the same factors we consider when breeding for Conformation. The two main areas are soundness and temperament. Far too many breedings take place because two dogs have done well in Obedience with little consideration given to the background of the dogs or whether the breeding will result in quality get. As an example, if both dogs are minimally overshot, it may pose no problem for them, but the combination could prove disastrous to the offspring, and that breeding should not be undertaken.

STRUCTURE

Because *soundness* is important to the well-being of any dog, anyone who breeds dogs, for whatever purpose, would be well-advised to learn as much as possible about canine structure and movement. Why do some horses have a smooth, comfortable trot and others rattle the rider's teeth even at a slow trot? *Structure* is why. And it is this structure that enables the horse to cover ground smoothly without tiring or to clear a jump effortlessly.

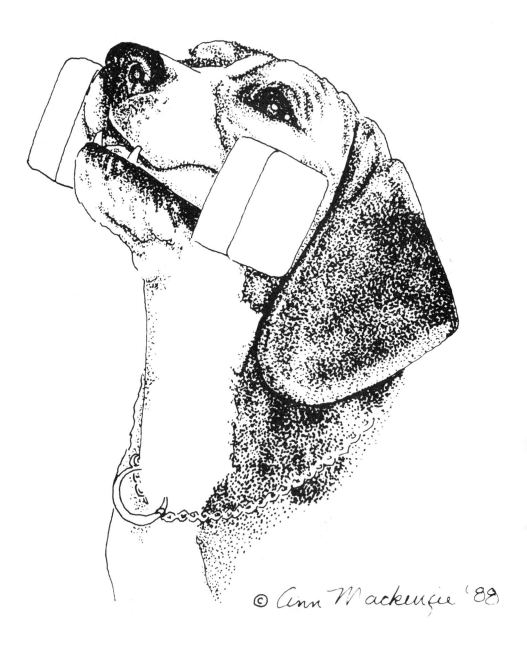

© Ann Mackenzie '88

Ch. Teloca Sirius Morningstar, UD, finding the scent articles that had been handled by owner/trainer. *Robin Whitelock*

Ch. Teloca Sirius Honor Bright, CDX, nine years old, enjoying the leap over the broad jump. *Robin Whitelock*

Why are we discussing horses, you may wonder? Many Obedience exhibitors do not seem to realize that their dogs are working animals just like horses. Structure can make their work easy or impossibly difficult.

Everyone knows about hip dysplasia; often, however, too little consideration is given to other important factors. Consider the dog with improper shoulder layback. In Advanced Obedience on a three-day weekend, this dog could be required to clear a jump fifteen times. Since straight shoulders do not permit it to bend its legs easily and cushion its landings, its shoulders and legs take an unbelievable amount of abuse. Eventually, the dog will turn up lame or will refuse the jumps "for no apparent reason." This may explain why a dog with a leg or two in Utility is suddenly retired. Investigation may uncover a dog whose poor structure has finally caught up with him. The pain may have become so intense that he cannot continue to jump. Time and training have been wasted, and that longed-for Utility title is beyond grasp.

To breed for proper structure, we must understand what it is and why it is important. Many good books have been written on the subject, such as Rachel Page Elliott's *The New Dogsteps* (New York: Howell Book House, 1983), and they are of great value to the breeder.

Before choosing to breed, we will want to observe the *movement* of the potential dam and sire, both on walking on lead at a show gait and running free. If possible, we will watch them both jump. Their movement should be strong and free, without restriction. A strong rear with good drive makes the takeoff to the jump easier. A dog that skips or hops may have slipped stifles— not necessarily a crippling problem, but one that may interfere with jumping. Arthritis or spinal problems on either side of the pedigree should be identified.

In many breeds, including Beagles, "More is Better" is the rule of the day when it comes to bone. This is certainly not true in a dog that is expected to perform athletic feats. Add heavy bone to a dog with moderately straight shoulders, and you have trouble. Instead, for the parents of our future "High in Trial" dog, let's choose a dam and sire with moderate bone, good shoulder layback and proper turn of stifle. Let's watch them move. Look for feet or hocks that turn in or out. Look for sidewinding or crabbing. Any of these factors will weaken a dog and cause it to tire more easily. Continued jumping of an unsound dog with the resultant concussion can ultimately cause complete breakdown of the dog's front assembly.

TEMPERAMENT

Now, ideally, we have found partners with proper structure. Next, we will consider the other most important factor: *temperament*. While it is obvious that a dog that is terribly shy or easily spooked will have problems in the obedience ring, other personality traits can help or hinder our future star. In our opinion, the perfect temperament for an Obedience dog is one that is alert, attentive, willing to please and stout of heart.

It is easy to see how our curious, independent, lounge-lizard hounds have gotten a bad rap in the Obedience world. No, we are referring to "working dogs," who have been bred for generations to hang on their masters' every word. However, some careful selection can improve the likelihood that our dog will pay attention and get the job done handily.

Again, observation is a key. How do the prospective parents relate to people and other animals? We would choose parents who prefer the company of humans to other canines. Many Obedience experts will not bother with a dog that will not play with people, and we consider this important. After all, aren't we going to expect these pups to play some very complicated games?

Too much submission or dominance presents its own set of problems. A dog that is very submissive is not likely to stand up well to the constant correct-and-praise of Obedience training. It may also have trouble with the stress of new environments and with new people and dogs. While the dominant and even aggressive dog can be trained and may end up being a good worker, getting and keeping its respect may present a real problem. (See the information on the Campbell Puppy Behavior Test in Chapter 11, "Puppy Training for Home and Show Ring.")

Is it possible to breed dogs that perform well in Obedience and also approximate the breed Standard sufficiently to show in Conformation? We believe that it is not only possible, but highly desirable. The basic structure needed for Obedience is the same that produces a dog that moves properly in the breed ring.

The temperament desired in an Obedience dog makes for a good show dog.

The past record illustrates that it is indeed possible to successfully show the same dog in both Conformation and Obedience. A prime example is Anne Schaefer's Ch. Daisyrun Benbrae Dauntless, CDX, who completed her championship requirements and Companion Dog title at the same time. She was then shown as a champion while working on her Companion Dog Excellent title. The result? One weekend, this lovely bitch, owner-handled, was awarded a Hound Group Third on Saturday, awarded a Second Place in Open A on Sunday, and selected Best of Variety, fifteen-inch, at the 1987 National Beagle Club of America Specialty.

In fact, training and showing in Obedience can provide the show dog with confidence and stability. We have shown several dogs in both Conformation and Obedience at the same time.

Ch. Teloca Pruf O'the Puddin', CD, attained his Companion Dog title while being campaigned as a champion. Ch. Teloca Honor Bright, CDX, and Teloca Sirius Rhedd Butler, CDX, finished their CD and championship titles at the same time, and each went on to earn a CDX while being campaigned.

Ch. Teloca Sirius Morningstar, UD, TD, TT, matured more slowly, so he got his CD while we waited for him to grow up. He then completed his

The one-minute sit during class at an armory. If the third beagle from the right looks a little bored, it is probably because the routine is "old hat" for this fourteen-year-old. *Robin Whitelock*

Ch. Teloca Sirius Rhedd Butler, CD, fifteen inches, owned by Rosalind Hall and Marie Shuart, has fully demonstrated its aptitude for both conformation and Obedience competition. He was Reserve Winners Dog at the National Beagle Club Specialty, 1988 among other noteworthy honors. *Earl Graham*

UD, passed the American Temperament Test, earned a Tracking title, and spent several years doing pet therapy at a high school and a retirement home.

We have found that the care taken in breeding for stable temperament is beneficial in another field, as two Teloca Beagles were selected to work for the United States Department of Agriculture's Beagle Brigade. Ch. Teloca Jussie's Girl and Ch. Teloca Sheik Rattle and Roll have the "merry little Beagle" temperament that makes them nonthreatening to travelers as they sniff luggage for contraband food and plants. To do this important work, they must be impervious to the noises and confusion of one the busiest airports in the United States.

Although heredity is not the only important factor in good temperament, we consider it very important. Many of the Beagles currently being shown in Obedience were chosen by their owners partly because of the number of Obedience titles in their pedigrees.

TRAINING

Although every Beagle will not be shown for a formal Obedience title, we do believe that they would all benefit from basic Obedience training. A dog that sits, stays and, most important, comes when called is a more pleasant and safe member of a household. Many dog clubs, as well as private trainers, offer household Obedience classes. Most of these classes use motivational techniques and teach the owner how to train his or her own dog. We prefer these classes to private training, as they teach the dog to obey in the presence of distractions from other people and dogs.

What do we do with the pups we have chosen for future Obedience careers? We do not begin formal Obedience training with very young puppies. However, there are many games and activities we can enjoy with them that will enhance their later training. Teaching a pup to fetch a favorite toy and to come to you for a treat or a pat are good starters. Any game that causes the pup to focus its attention on you will help it learn to concentrate on your commands later. We feel that the more of this type of human attention a pup receives at a young age, the easier its later training will be.

Using our Beagles' natural "chow hound" tendency and techniques of shaping behavior with positive reinforcement, you can teach a young pup to respond to cues, but remember that its attention span is very short, so training sessions should be kept short, and only positive reinforcement should be used.

Marie uses a correction-and-praise method of training, while Rosalind uses motivational shaping to teach exercises and both positive reinforcement and correction once the dog knows the exercises. Both methods work successfully. There are many good Obedience training books on the market, and many authors present seminars in which they explain their methods and work with handlers and dogs. We have found these seminars very useful in our own work, and we are constantly searching for new and better ways to train.

Ch. Teloca It's Only Money, fifteen-inch dog (Ch. Lanbur Coupe De Ville ex Ch. Teloca Happy Face), shown working with its owner-trainer, Marie Shuart. *Booth*

U-CD Gabriel's Chelsea Morning Star, CDX, TDX, CGC, TDI, Can CD, fifteen-inch bitch (Gabriel Baal ex Jolene Joy), owned by Denise Nord, working in Novice Agility class. *Karen MacDonald*

Chelsea, the only Beagle to have won an all-breed High in Trial, negotiates the "dog walk" in the Novice Agility class. *Karen MacDonald*

Choosing a training method and an instructor can be key to your success. If an instructor tells you you're wasting your time trying to train a Beagle, obviously you are in the wrong place. Before adopting any training method, you should understand it thoroughly. For a method to work well, you must be comfortable with it. Before you sign up for a class, observe it a few times. Do the dogs seem to be improving? Do the handlers seem to understand and follow the instructor's directions? Are there enough instructors and helpers for the size of the class, or do some handlers seem to be neglected or lost? Does the instructor adapt training to the size and temperament of each dog, or are a shy Sheltie and an aggressive Doberman treated the same way? Does the overall method of training suit your personality? If you can't find an instructor you are comfortable with, it may be better to read a few books and go it alone.

Whatever training method you use, it is extremely important that you assume an unquestioned position as "pack leader." Our little hounds are very quick to take advantage of anyone they perceive as an "easy mark." We are patient when teaching a new exercise, but once the dog knows what is being asked of it, a quick collar correction is given if it fails to respond to a command. Every correction is followed with praise so that the dog will know we are pleased with it for finally obeying our command. If you choose food as a reinforcer, it may take extra time to wean a Beagle off the constant reward and develop a reliable behavior in a ring setting. A Beagle will do almost anything for a treat but is quick to realize that you can't use food in actual trial conditions, so this type of training can backfire unless great care is taken. Losing one's temper or using nagging corrections brings out spite and stubborness in most dogs, especially hounds. Consistency and praise usually produce happy, dependable workers.

WHAT OBEDIENCE OFFERS

Obedience training and exhibiting offer an avenue of accomplishment and companionship with our dogs. The American Kennel Club has structured this activity so that it is available to everyone, whether the goal is a Companion Dog title on a retired show dog or a Utility degree with class wins and High in Trial quests.

Admittedly, it may be difficult to train a Beagle for the quality of performance needed to achieve the high scores required for placements. However, the degree of difficulty is matched only by the feeling of pride and satisfaction when, having placed in a difficult class, you are standing out front with your Beagle among the Obedience breeds.

Of course, there are pitfalls. Training for excellence can produce an intensity that takes all the fun out of exhibiting. And our little hounds seem to sense this. It leads to severe cases of canine amnesia, during which a UD Beagle forgets what the word "heel" means. Or, being natural clowns, they may resort

My Regal Beagle Amanda, CDX, TDX, fifteen-inch bitch (Ch. Bridal Vale's Beowulf Moody Blue ex Ellie's Cassandra), owned and trained by Martha Ciaschini, shown winning High in Trial, 1995 NBC Specialty. *Tom di Giacomo*

to comedy and create new and clever ways of performing the exercises. One of our dogs left the ring and climbed into a friendly lap ringside, where it doubtlessly felt it would find sympathy.

We do strive for the best possible performance that each dog is capable of on a particular day, but we try to do that maintaining our sense of humor and our knowledge that whatever our dog might do has probably been done before.

For most of us, the championship title is the end to a dog's competitive career. While we may go on to breed our champion, he or she is basically retired. Obedience training and exhibiting can add continued years of companionship and enjoyment for both dog and owner.

In 1995, the AKC accepted a new performance event called Agility. Agility is a sport that began about fifteen years ago in England, and while not formally an Obedience event, it requires an obedient dog. In Agility, the dog is required to run an obstacle course consisting of various jumps, tunnels, a teeter-totter and other "contact obstacles" within a specified time. This sport has quickly become very popular, because it is fun and challenging. Many Beagles are participating successfully in AKC and other types of Agility.

chapter 6

The Beagle as a Pet

Beagles are not for everyone—but almost. Not only the personality, but the packaging of this little scent hound make it an ideal breed as a house companion. The only thing better than one Beagle is two!

PERSONALITY

Friendly, outgoing and into everything as a young dog, the Beagle matures into an affectionate and active adult. The combination of a gentle, pleading expression with an enormous curiosity is comical. Beagles are natural clowns. It is hard to be downhearted with a Beagle around.

Unfortunately, many of the qualities that make the Beagle an ideal companion also make it an ideal experimental animal. Beagle colonies in veterinary research centers abound. The hound's generally docile nature, eagerness to please, lack of aggressive response to handling, adaptability to people and other dogs and sturdiness of health—characteristics of the breed—lead to their use in research.

Unlike some breeds that bond with one family member, Beagles bond to all, especially children. Kids smell good, play and run—all aspects a Beagle loves. Friendly almost to a fault, the Beagle is not an independent dog. There is always "important business" that the Beagle must attend to—checking the yard to see what interesting smells may have developed overnight, inspecting the kitchen refrigerator when the door is opened to determine what good things might be stashed inside and finding out what that *is* on the other side of the fence.

Some Beagles dig and climb. Some bark. They may appear stubborn. Their sense of smell is so keen that when it is focused in on an interesting trail, repeated attempts to get their attention may be necessary. They will roam if not properly fenced.

PHYSICAL CHARACTERISTICS

The Beagle is a short-haired, small- to medium-size scent hound. Adult thirteen-inchers weigh between thirteen and twenty pounds, and fifteen-inchers can weigh up to twenty-eight pounds. Shedding does occur, particularly in the spring.

Its gentle facial expression, framed by long ears, and a very appealing demeanor a give the aspect of a perpetual puppy. People are always asking about your white-faced, dark-eyed fourteen-year-old: "How old is your puppy?"

REQUIREMENTS OF A GOOD HOME

"I only sleep in the house . . . ." All dogs deserve good homes: a loving family, safe environment, proper food and health care, regular exercise and essential obedience training. Beagles have some particular needs. Generally, children under five or six are too young for a Beagle puppy. Accidents can and do happen with injuries to the small, active puppy.

Easily bored, a young Beagle requires companionship in the form of a regular daily exercise/play schedule and if possible, another canine or feline friend. If left unattended for long periods of time, a Beagle is likely to develop into a creative destroyer. Excavated gardens, holes under fencing, shredded patio furniture, and neighbors distraught with "Beagle barking" make life miserable for both dog and owner. If left outside at night, a Beagle is more likely than not to bark to the point of annoyance.

So sleeping in the house is a necessity. A comfy crate or special spot in the kitchen or utility room works nicely. A safe, confined area, particularly for a puppy or young Beagle, keeps everyone happy. Of course, the Beagle's first choice is with you in your bed. If the bed-sharing arrangement is not for you, don't start it!

A BAD HABIT

Probably the most unpleasant habit a Beagle has is the result of its ability to eat anything and everything. Consequently, stool-eating occurs with some frequency, particularly if there are several Beagles in the household. Occasionally, a single Beagle will recycle its own droppings.

There are more hypotheses regarding possible causes than there are cures. Reasons given range from sheer boredom to nutritional deficiencies. Our guess is that they simply like it. Not all Beagles recycle, but a significant number do.

Bad breath, ingestion of parasites and weight gain can result.

Efforts to combat *coprophagia*—a fancy term for stool eating—include picking up immediately after defecation; placing an unpleasant-tasting additive, such as Adolph's Meat Tenderizer, on the stool prior to attempted ingestion; and adding a multivitamin, garlic or enzyme obtained from your veterinarian to the daily ration that makes the stool unpalatable.

Good luck!

Ch. Skyline's Rumor Has It at three months with friend Matt Forbes. *Kathy Forbes*

A "Just-Wright" puppy learning to be irresistable. *Julie Wright*

Rancho Glen's Crackerjack, thirteen-inch dog, owned by Michael and Mary Lynne Katusich, at age fourteen can still play chase with one of his bunny neighbors. *Katusich*

chapter 7

So You Want to Show and Breed Beagles

Most of us began with just an "ordinary" Beagle. From there, it is a natural step to start observing other Beagles. Local dog shows provide an opportunity to see Beagles from different lines and to meet various breeders.

Each year, hundreds of AKC-licensed all-breed shows are held throughout the United States. Conformation classes are offered for each of the breeds. To earn a Conformation Championship, a dog must win a total of fifteen points, including two major wins (three to five points each) under at least three different judges. The majors cannot be under the same judge. The point scale is determined regionally by the number of dogs defeated; this number varies in different zones of the country, based on the previous year's entry for the breed in that region and determined by the American Kennel Club. The applicable point rating is published in every dog show catalog.

Classes at the shows are divided by sex, age and special categories, with six months being the minimum age of eligibility. In Beagles, there is also a division into two varieties: less than thirteen inches and more than thirteen inches and not exceeding fifteen inches at the shoulder, with the measurement made from the ground or floor to the tops of the shoulders.

Currently, the Winners Dog and Winners Bitch (best nonchampion in each sex) compete for Best of Winners and also against the champions for Best of Variety. The two variety winners are then eligible to compete in the Hound Group. The winner of the Hound Group competes against the other six Group winners for Best in Show.

A Specialty Show is a Conformation Show (with or without Obedience classes) for a single breed. The same AKC rules apply here as well. Here, the two variety winners compete against each other for Best of Breed, unless the Specialty is held in conjunction with the regular classes at an all-breed show.

After the decision is made to obtain a good conformation prospect, here are some important suggestions you must bear in mind:

Ch. Craftsman of Walnut Hall, fifteen inches, owned by Mrs. Harkness Edwards. *The Beagle Yearbook*, 1942.

Four generations of Kinsman Beagles. From left: Ch. Kinsman Little Merryman, Int. Ch. Kinsman Jimmy Valentine, Int. Ch. Travis Court Terwillegar and Int. Ch. Kinsman High Jinks.

WHAT TO LOOK FOR

For us, the most important quality to look for is temperament. A good conformation Beagle is outgoing, friendly and has a "look at me" attitude. Additionally, you will want a nonaggressive hound that will get along with other dogs as well as people. Long after its showing and breeding days are over, you will want a Beagle with which you can enjoy living.

Second in importance are *type* and *soundness*. Hopefully, the two will go together. The hound must *look like a Beagle*. There are many "looks" in good Beagle type from which to choose. This is strictly a personal choice on which excellent lines have been based. A good linebred or inbred individual generally produces more predictable, consistent get than would an outcross.

Ch. Shaw's Share The Spirit, thirteen-inch bitch (Ch. Shaw's Mikey Likes It ex Ch. Echo Run Kindred Spirit), owned by John and Peggy Shaw, was BOB at the Central Illinois and Wisconsin Beagle Club Specialties, 1995, and BOV, NBC Specialty 1996. *Ashbey*

Dutch & Luxemb. Ch. Sergeant Pepper's Road Junction (right), Group Winner and Holland's Beagle of the Year, with Int., Belg. & Luxemb.Ch. Sergeant Pepper Go Go Go. Owned by Baroness van der Borch tot Verwolde.

HOW TO FIND YOUR BEAGLE

Read. Read Chapter 2, "The Beagle Standard," and as many books about the breed as are readily available. Look at as many pictures of Beagles, old and current, as you can get your hands on. Local kennel clubs often provide lists of breeders within their areas. The National Beagle Club of America provides names of member breeders by region upon request. (Write to American Kennel Club, 51 Madison Ave., New York NY 10010 for name and address of the Club Secretary.) Visit local breeders and write to others. Most likely, the look of one or two lines will appeal to you. But ask questions: How long can you expect this Beagle to live? What health and genetic problems are encountered in this line? And if you intend to breed, are the bitches in the line easy whelpers? A good foundation bitch is always the cornerstone of any breeding program.

The purchase of a good hound as your first Beagle can offer you much-needed experience in conditioning, training, grooming and handling. For the serious novice, the purchase of a second Beagle usually comes within two to three years.

After you make the decision to breed a line of your own, a plan is essential. Revisions in that plan will most likely occur as circumstances dictate; for example, an eagerly-awaited outcross litter may uncover a previously absent genetic problem, or that special stud dog may suddenly becomes sterile. But the goal of a good breeding program (the production of good-natured, sound Beagles of correct type) does not change—only the route to that goal changes.

HOME AND KENNEL FACILITIES

Home Sweet Home—most of us begin with a house built for people. The Beagles come later. It certainly is possible to operate a small breeding program within your home, but local animal-control regulations, proximity and type of neighbors and your ability to care for and supervise your Beagles are important considerations. Raising a Beagle as a house dog makes for the best temperament, personality development and training. Though innately eager to please its human friends, the hound can't learn the house rules by being relegated to the "back forty" with little human contact. Adjustable gates for doorways or pass-throughs save many a repainting job and provide the Beagle puppy with a view of the household without risk of accident. Crate training, a safe, secured indoor area (kitchen, laundry room and so on) and an adequate outdoor exercise yard are essentials.

Gardens make poor exercise yards for Beagles. Easy access to pesticides, snail bait and toxic plants leads to dangerously ill animals. The potential damage to your garden is reason enough to Beagle-proof the area. Excavating to China is marvelous fun for the puppy but not for the hardworking gardener. A fenced run with access to an enclosed area within the garage, for example, works beautifully. Beagles can be climbers and diggers, so fences need to be at least six feet high and buried deep into the ground. Laying chicken wire or similar mesh bent at a right angle, with the vertical portion attached to the bottom of the fence and the horizontal section extending below the ground into the exercise area for three or four feet, should defeat even the most enterprising of excavators. The surface of the yard needs to be of material that can be easily cleaned and disinfected. Concrete or certain types of flat rock work well. Unfortunately, some Beagles are inveterate gravel-grazers, so a footing of pea gravel should be avoided.

Of course, provisions for shade, shelter and plenty of cool water are mandatory. Whatever you work out, the local climate and kind of house you live in will determine what works best for quartering your Beagles. Some homes have large basements that serve well in cold winters. But remember, Beagles who live in basements are deprived of sunlight, fresh air and opportunities to learn about new sights, smells, sounds and people. Also, the logistics of disinfecting and cleaning basement kennels can be challenging.

Seldom mentioned is the fact that the people living in your home need to have some living space away from the dogs if they so wish. Not all your friends love to share dinner with one or several hungry hounds.

If I Only Had a Kennel . . .

Kennel facilities certainly make life easier. There is one problem. Because Beagles are pack dogs and get along well with one another, it is far too easy to keep more hounds than is sensible. The population seems to expand in direct relationship to the available space. How many breeding kennels have you visited with an empty run or two?

What works best in respect to kennels depends on where you live and the climate. Neighbors close enough to be disturbed by Beagles barking at night mean the construction of a relatively soundproof kennel building. Ideally, there should be plenty of light, air, exposure to everyday noises and lots of human activity. Concrete floors make for easy cleanup. Pass-throughs between inside and outside runs can be equipped with flap or guillotine doors.

We prefer a good grade of wire fencing where the wires run vertically and horizontally. Though chain link is wonderfully durable, its diagonal pattern produces a narrow angle where Beagle toenails can easily get caught and torn off.

Outside runs should be partially roofed over to afford shelter and shade, and a raised sleeping pad of wood or heavy plastic should be provided. At least one or two completely covered runs are useful for bitches in season or to prevent the occasional climber from visiting adjacent runs.

Sleeping quarters pose somewhat of a problem. Many Beagles mark their sleeping areas by urinating on them. Some breeders use a box containing cedar shavings or hay that can be replaced. Sleeping areas should be raised from the concrete flooring, facilitating cleaning. We and our Beagles are great

Ch. Vinla's Midnight Maverick, thirteen-inch dog (Ch. Aggie's Hot Apple Tart ex Ch. Jam's TL), Group and Specialty winner, owned by Kevin and Darla Brooks. Sire of fifteen champions, he was the thirteen-inch BOV at the 1994 and 1995 NBC Specialty Shows and an Award of Merit Winner, NBC Specialty 1996. *Kohler*

Ch. Nieland's Lucky Lady, thirteen-inch bitch (Ch. Sureluv's Fran-Ray's Bandit ex Ch. Mill Creek Dumplin' O'Lanbur), a Best in Show and multi-Group winner, owned by Janet and Bill Nieland. *Ludwig*

enthusiasts for double-strength cardboard banana boxes, which we place on wooden platforms. The Beagles love the enclosed feeling of the boxes, three or four frequently cramming into one box! When bored, they can always dig in and chew on them without deleterious effect.

Ideally, a kennel room containing a sink (large enough for Beagle bathing), a small refrigerator, cupboards, storage space for food, shelves and space for grooming table and crates polishes off the structure.

Your kennel should have a heating and cooling system.

A large dirt or grass-covered exercise area into which the kennel opens provides the Beagles with plenty of room to run. Whether your hounds will use all that space depends on its shape and what stimulation for activity exists. Many breeders have invested in large fencing expenditures only to find all their Beagles heaped up around the entrance closest to the house, just waiting for their next meal. Rectangular yards don't work as well as U-shaped or irregularly-shaped ones. With a U-shaped yard surrounding the kennel building, the Beagles have to run from one side to the other to check out the action.

Of course, plenty of fresh water and shade should be available in the exercise area.

Perimeter fencing has to be high enough to discourage climbing and imbedded deep enough to thwart the digging Beagle. Sleeping or sitting pads off the ground add to the attraction for the dogs. The large, wooden spools used for telephone cables make ideal platforms for rest or play or as observation posts.

Make your kennel setup as practical and convenient for you and your dogs as possible. Clean completely daily, pick up as often as necessary and disinfect regularly with a rotating schedule of Clorox, iodine scrub, Roccal and Nolvasan.

Instructions regarding feeding, medications and the cleaning routine, plus the name, address and phone number of your veterinarian(s) should be posted in your kennel whenever you are away from home for an extended period of time or in the event of sudden emergency. Another thought: Make provisions in your will for financing the care and disposition of your dogs, with a particular individual responsible for administering these provisions.

YOUR BREEDING PROGRAM

Luck plays an important part in any successful breeding program. A fortunate combination of genes enables an exceptional stud or brood bitch to produce consistently excellent get. Consider yourself blessed to have one of these producers.

What *is* within a breeder's control is the selection of stock to be used. A satisfactory bitch puppy from a line known for consistent quality in its bitches is a better choice than an outstanding one from a line known for mediocre-producing bitches, and a male Beagle whose get from a variety of bitches shows his consistent excellence is the best bet as a stud.

The pedigree and appearance of your foundation Beagle determine the next step. Cementing the virtues within a good line while weeding out the faults is everyone's goal, and while this can be done over several generations, there comes a time when new blood is needed—for example, to restore vigor and bone and to increase fertility.

Not infrequently, however, new problems may arise from these out-crosses. Sometimes, a genetic dead end results. Such was the case with one of our better show bitches. With a little luck, however, the Beagles from a first-generation outcross, when bred back into either line, will reproduce well.

The choice of which line to use as foundation stock and which Beagle stud to use may not be easy. Some breeders opt for the top winner of the day. If the stud chosen also happens to be a fine producer, as was Ch. Starbuck's Hang 'Em High, the results can be excellent. But not all top-winning confor-mation Beagles reproduce in kind. Here, a stud of proven ability but with a more modest win record might serve your bitch far better.

There really is no single right way to breed good Beagles. Many routes to the same end exist. A breeder may get consistently good conformation Beagles while breeding to successive top-winning males. Others outcross fre-quently but to Beagles of the same general appearance with successful results. We (JM and AM) pursued a program of very close linebreeding as well as inbreeding a time or two and had a good run for our money for a number of years.

Conventional wisdom dictates that new gene pools are necessary after three or four generations. A look at a cross-section of current Beagle pedi-grees indicates a shrinking of our conformation pool. This is probably why we are seeing an increase in certain genetic problems.

Frankness among cooperating breeders about particular unwanted recessives can make for more carefully planned breedings based on better information.

Ch. Teloca Patches Littl' Dickens, thirteen-inch dog (Ch. Teloca Patches On Target ex Ch. Teloca Upstage Bann'd in Boston, CD), a multiple BIS, Group and Specialty winner; sire of three BIS and many Group winners; Beagle of the Year, NBC, 1984 and 1985; thirteen-inch Beagle of the Year, NBC, 1986. Owned by Wade Burns and Jon Woodring. *Graham*

Blackspot Some Like It Hot, fifteen-inch dog (Arg. Ch. Harrowill's Alien ex Ch. Blackspot Tessie), owned by Ruben and Monica Sosa Quiroga of Argentina.

chapter 8

A Breeder's Notebook

Note: All Beagles earmarked as potential breeding stock should be screened for hip dysplasia, inherited eye problems, von Willebrand's Disease, thyroid function and brucellosis prior to breeding. (See Chapter 16, "Your Beagle's Health and Genetics.")

MANAGEMENT OF THE BROOD BITCH

Good reproductive care of your potential brood bitch begins long before its first breeding. Priscilla Stockner, DVM, recommends that between seven and ten months of age, prior to its first season, your puppy bitch should have a good physical examination, a blood panel, urinalysis, brucellosis serum titre and thyroid function tests. The vaginal examination, both digital and visual, with smear and culture, will uncover any physical anomalies or obstacles to breeding and potential for infection. It is a bit disconcerting to discover at the time of breeding that your eager Beagles are unable to consummate their "marriage." Persistent hymens do occur.

Vaginal Cultures

Thirty percent to 40 percent of vaginal cultures from healthy bitches, taken midcycle, will not grow out any organisms. With the onset of a season, bacterial growth will flourish, however. Therefore a repeat smear and culture need to be done during early proestrus. Certain bacteria are disease-producing, and if found, must be treated. Heavy growth of *E. coli*, if untreated, will lead to pyometra (infected uterus) by four years of age. Eighty percent of bitches so infected are infertile. Beta-hemolytic streptococcus flourishing in the vagina reduces the chances of pregnancy, slows sperm motility and leads to 80 percent of neonatal deaths.

Ch. Kings Creek Triple Threat, fifteen-inch dog (Ch. Kings Creek Stagerlee ex Security Susie Black Flash), first Best of Breed at the NBC Club Specialty, 1970; multiple Best in Show wins and four Bests of Variety, Westminster Kennel Club. Sire of 78 champions, owned by Marcia Foy. *Evelyn Shafer*

Head study of Ch. Duke Sinatra, fifteen-inch dog, BIS winner in the 1940s, owned by Mrs. R.G. Hess.

Obviously, it is vitally important to recognize such problems early. Douching once daily with the appropriate antibiotic solution for varying lengths of time can control these organisms. If there is no veterinary reproductive specialist in your area, your veterinarian can work in consultation with one at a distance to give you the best support.

Brucellosis

Brucellosis titres are essential *prior* to each breeding. *Brucella canis*, the organism causing brucellosis, is spread by both oral and genital contact. Sterility in the male and spontaneous abortion in the female are consequences of this infection. Highly contagious, the organism can be contracted from contaminated ground. Until recently, the diagnosis of brucellosis meant castration and spaying, if not euthanasia, for the affected dogs. However, treatment with a combination of long-term antibiotic therapy has been effective in some experimental programs.

Thyroid Function

Repeat blood tests for thyroid function should be done prior to each season. See Chapter 16 for further details on your Beagle's health and genetics.

Parasite Control

An ongoing parasite control program is essential with your Beagles. Fleas, hookworm and whipworm thrive in hot, humid climates. Coccidia abound, and Giardia is becoming more common. And, of course, the incidence of heartworm is now nation-wide, if not global. Stool checks and specific medications for each of these conditions, plus specific instructions for disinfecting the environment, may be obtained from your veterinarian. The alternative to routine use of a heartworm preventative is a twice-yearly blood test. If the test is positive, then the dog is treated.

Once your bitch is bred, it is too late to launch an extensive extermination effort. Whatever goes in or on her for treatment can adversely affect the developing fetuses.

Encysted roundworm larvae in the dam may be released at about forty-five days of the pregnancy into the placenta, thus infecting the puppies. Hookworm infestation of young puppies can be very dangerous.

Feeding

Contrary to popular opinion, dieting your bitch prior to her season and breeding is not the best route to a successful pregnancy. On the other hand, a grossly overweight Beagle isn't a good candidate for motherhood.

Experiments suggest that increasing food intake by 10 percent with the beginning of its season until breeding and then returning to normal food intake after breeding increases the chances of conception. There is some evidence that overfeeding after breeding leads to a drop in fertility.

Meat, chicken, cottage cheese, egg yolk and fish added in small amounts to a good basic dog food provide an excellent source of animal protein. Raw liver, one tablespoon three times a week, ensures an adequate amount of zinc, which is necessary for healthy, vigorous newborns. Total fat content of the diet for a pregnant bitch should not exceed 15 percent.

The dam's intake will need to be increased gradually, beginning with the fifth week after breeding. The amount required will be determined by the size of the litter. Maintaining about one-half inch of subcutaneous fat over the rib cage is ideal for a Beagle. The expectant bitch will be more comfortable during the last two to three weeks of her pregnancy, particularly if she is carrying a large number of pups, if her daily ration is divided into two meals. Some bitches lose their appetites a few days before whelping, but most continue to be absolutely ravenous until labor commences!

Once nursing begins, your bitch will require additional food, the amount once again determined by the number of nursing puppies. Adequate nutrition is absolutely essential to good milk production. Phyllis Holst, DVM, recommends one-and-a-half times the normal intake for the first week, two times for the second, and three times from the third to the sixth week. Animal protein, added in small amounts daily, and vitamin-mineral supplements continue for the duration of nursing. Bitches fed adequately do not need to suffer weight loss.

Ch. Windholme's Bangle, the first Beagle to become a Best in Show winner. *The Beagle in America and England*, H. W. Prentice

Ch. Altopa Atom, thirteen inches, dual-purpose Beagle owned by O.J. Gennett in the late 1940s.

Vitamin-Mineral Supplementation

If your bitch is not already on a good general vitamin-mineral supplement, begin her on one at about four weeks after breeding and continue through the period of lactation. Some specially designed dog food for pregnant bitches contains all they need.

Calcium-phosphorus-vitamin D additives are no longer considered essential. Indeed, the additives may *decrease* the bitch's ability to deal with the calcium requirements of nursing.

Boosters

No medication (with the exception of that for heartworm control) should be given during pregnancy. If, for some reason, antibiotics are required, only those safe for pregnant bitches and developing puppies are to be used and under supervision of your veterinarian.

MANAGEMENT OF THE STUD DOG

As with the care of the brood bitch, an ounce of prevention is worth a ton of cure.

There have been a number of good conformation Beagle males in the past thirty years that have become infertile after siring only one to two litters. Diagnostic studies done after the fact indicate that some, if properly treated early enough, may not have become permanently sterile.

A good general physical and genital examination of the young male, nine to twelve months old, is a must. This workup should also include a blood panel, thyroid level and a brucellosis titre. Examination of the genitals, observation of breeding behavior and a semen check complete the picture.

Semen should *always* be collected in the presence of a "teaser" bitch;[1] without its presence, false negatives sometimes occur. The three portions of the semen (first and third portions are prostatic fluid, normally clear, the second is milky in color and contains sperm) are examined microscopically. Number, shape and motility of the sperm provide a baseline with which future counts can be compared. Semen examination should be repeated yearly.

Prior to each breeding, a blood brucellosis titre should be obtained.

Normal thyroid function is necessary for sperm production. Early diagnosis and treatment of hypothryroidism (inadequate thyroid hormone production) can make a difference between temporary and permanent infertility.

Chronic prostatitis, usually bacterial in nature, also affects sperm production. Copious urination, in contrast to the usual or normal marking pattern, and smaller, flatter stools may indicate enlargement of the infected prostate gland. Again, the earlier the treatment, the better the chance that the infertility can be reversed.

---

[1]*In lieu of a teaser bitch to aid in obtaining a sperm specimen, cotton balls saturated with vaginal discharge of a bitch in season that have been frozen immediately can be used as a substitute. When needed, remove one of the balls from the freezer and let the male smell it as the specimen is obtained.*

Ch. Meadow Crest Harmony, thirteen-inch bitch (Ch. White Acres I'm Heavenly Too ex Ch. Validay's Maestro's Cristina), Specialty thirteen-inch Variety winner and Group placer, owned by Annette Didier. *Booth*

THOSE FEMALE SEX HORMONES AT WORK

Poor timing in a breeding accounts for 25 percent of missed conceptions. The remaining 75 percent of missed conceptions are due to problems with low fertility or infertility. Early diagnosis and treatment of the latter may reverse the situation.

If you, like the rest of us, are forgetful, a quick review of the reproductive physiology of the bitch is always in order.

Ovarian Cycle

There are four phases of hormonal changes and associated behavior in the bitch:

1. *Anestrus*, the resting phase, is characterized by absence of reproductive activity. Vaginal smears show only a few nonsuperficial cells, white blood cells and occasionally a few old, superficial cells. Progesterone levels are low. Duration of this phase can vary from one month to twelve months.

2. *Proestrus*, the beginning of reproductive activity, is accompanied by a gradual swelling of the vulva, a serosanguineous discharge (a combination of a thin, clear fluid colored with blood) and an increasing blood level of estradiol. The average length of this phase is about nine days, but it can vary from zero to seventeen days.

3. *Estrus* is that period during which the bitch is receptive to the male. The color of the vaginal discharge may or may not change and is *not* a reliable indicator of the onset of estrus. During this time, the bitch's vulva is full, and she will present her perineum (bottom) to the male, flagging her tail. Hormonally, this behavior occurs when blood levels of estradiol decrease and levels of progesterone increase. Luteinizing hormone ("a pituitary hormone with action on target cells in ovaries and teats," Phyllis Holst, DVM) is released in a surge over a period of twenty-four to forty-eight hours and leads to ovulation. *Ovulation*, the release of eggs, usually occurs within three days.

4. *Diestrus* lasts approximately sixty days and is the stage during which progesterone is the primary circulating hormone. This hormone leads to enlargement of breast tissue and activity of the lining of the uterus.

Discussion

All primary *oocytes*, the female reproductive cells, are produced over a twenty-four-hour period (Priscilla Stockner, DVM) and begin to descend through the *oviducts*, the tubes connecting the ovaries with the uterus. Three days are required for these eggs to be ready for fertilization. The egg's life span at that point is from twenty-four to forty-eight hours. Actual conception takes place three days after ovulation, when fertilization occurs in the lower end of the oviduct.

Vaginal smears reveal that maximum cornification is attained during late proestrus and early estrus. These large sheets of superficial cells persist until the end of estrus, the fertile period. Smears will not tell you when ovulation occurs except in retrospect. The length of time of full cornification varies from bitch to bitch, lasting from ten to fourteen days. For each individual bitch, however, the length of complete cornification (changes in size and shape of cells, indicating optimum breeding readiness) remains constant from season to season. A complete tracking of your bitch's estrus with serial vaginal smears can indicate a reliable pattern or schedule for future breedings.

A rise in serum progesterone level occurs with ovulation. After establishing your bitch's normal level during the first four to five days of its season, sampling every other day is sufficient to predict when ovulation has occurred. Breeding begins when the level exceeds 2 ng/ml (nanograms per milliliter) and is repeated every two to three days for a total of two or three breedings.

Not everyone will want to take the time and effort to visit the veterinarian for progesterone levels or serial slides or even to learn the technique of "doing it yourself." Therefore, a good rule of thumb is to first breed when the bitch is receptive and continue every other day until she declines or expresses her complete disgust with the poor stud who is still eager and more than willing.

Bitches bred two days after ovulation have the highest conception rates. However, successful breeding can occur in bitches bred from four days before to three days after ovulation. The best program is to breed six days, four days and two days before onset of diestrus. Since sperm can live as long as eleven days in the female reproductive tract, fertilization can occur even when the breedings may not be ideally timed. You can assume, however, that the fresher and more motile the sperm, the greater the likelihood of conception.

You don't need to worry about different degrees of maturity of the newborns, because all eggs are fertilized within a twenty-four hour period.

With the aid of this information, you will be able to time matings to maximize the chances of conception.

GETTING THE JOB DONE

Many Beagle bitches are as enthusiastic about being bred as they are about everything else. Occasionally, the level of pure abandon is so great that the actual mating can become a wrestling match involving Beagles and humans in the immediate vicinity. Since the hounds are relatively small and agile, breeding them fortunately does not require an army of assistants, as does breeding Bloodhounds or Bassets.

For the safety of the male and in the interest of saving time, two people, one small piece of carpet (large enough to accommodate two Beagles and two sets of knees) and perhaps some sterile KY Jelly are all that is needed in most instances.

Giving the two a few minutes of "foreplay" enables you to note the bitch's willingness to be bred and also gives the hounds, who may be strangers, an opportunity to get a little acquainted. Leads on each provide control in the event that the bitch is not quite ready and tries to defend her chastity by attempting to savage the stud.

Normal breeding behavior is characterized in a receptive bitch by enthusiastic play, sniffing the stud's penis, curling her tail to one side and presenting her vulva to him. Normal male behavior also includes play, licking the bitch's vulva and mounting her from the rear, clasping her "waist" with his forelegs and thrusting with his pelvis.

When it appears that penetration is about to happen, some assistance may be in order, with one person holding the bitch's head and front while the other

Ch. Rancho Glen's It's A Snap, fifteen-inch dog (Ch. Page Mill On The Road Again ex Ch. Ranah's Whimsy of Rancho Glen); a winner of the NBC Specialty, 1989, as well as a Group winner, pictured with one of his rabbit friends, owned by Michael and Mary Lynne Katusich. *Katusich*

gives the male an assist. Some studs, however, prefer to do it all by themselves and are put off by human help. Others, in their enthusiasm, may miss the mark by miles, literally hurling themselves completely over the bitch. We have found that the person at the working end can be of assistance by placing the left hand under the bitch from the left side with palm up and the index and middle fingers on either side of the vulva to serve as a support and guide for the penis. When penetration has occurred and active thrusting is taking place, the other hand can push the male gently into the bitch until a tie occurs.

Once a tie has been secured, the male can be turned.

Not all Beagle bitches are delighted with breeding. A strange environment, an unknown stud and the presence of a doting, talkative owner can disrupt the process. If the rear end of the bitch is obviously willing, as evidenced by flagging and tilting up of the pelvis, but the front is vociferously protesting, a soft, cloth belt or old pantyhose make an excellent muzzle. Tie either over the top of the bitch's muzzle, bring it back under its jaw, tie it again, and then loop it over the neck and tie it in a bow. This emergency muzzle should be loose enough to enable the bitch to open her mouth slightly to pant but tight enough to prevent her from snapping.

If all else fails, artificial insemination is an easy remedy. Since the AKC has approved the use of the technique by breeders in their own homes or kennels, it is a simple matter to obtain proper equipment. The technique is not difficult to master. There are excellent descriptions in both Phyllis Holst's book and Priscilla Stockner's articles.

The use of frozen semen and now cooled, fresh semen allows for a greater choice of stud dogs over a wider area and eliminates the stresses and risks involved in shipping bitches. With the increasing concern over contagious canine venereal diseases, artificial impregnation, routinely performed with cattle for many years, can be an added protection for the stud.

Remember that whenever we humans intercede in the process of canine reproduction, there is a risk that we may unwittingly perpetuate certain behavioral or physical problems.

THERE'S A BEAGLE IN THE OVEN

Diagnosis of Pregnancy

Eggs are fertilized about two days after ovulation as they reach the distal end of the oviduct. Division of cells begins, and implantation of the embryo in the uterine wall takes place about eighteen days post breeding (about seventeen days after ovulation). Whelping is most likely to occur fifty-six to fifty-eight days after the onset of diestrus or sixty-three days after breeding. Larger litters tend to be delivered a day or two earlier earlier.

Tiny embryos can be felt as early as nineteen days after the onset of diestrus but are best felt at twenty to twenty-eight days. Sonograms, used routinely by many veterinarians, provide a reliable, safe diagnostic confirmation. The visit to the veterinarian at this time also enables him or her to check for any potential problems.

Proper care of your pregnant bitch, as discussed earlier, also includes a checkup a week before her due date. Sonograms at this time may tell you the number and size of the puppies—information helpful in the management of the actual delivery. Arrangements for emergency coverage should be discussed with your veterinarian, because most bitches seem to deliver either late at night or during the wee hours of the morning. Unplanned visits to a strange emergency room in the middle of the night are not an ideal way to deliver a litter of puppies if assistance is required.

Preparing for Delivery

Whelping area: The first requirement is a quiet, warm room that is free from too much activity. We have found that the removable metal pan of a commercial whelping pen, lined with abundant paper, works well as the "delivery room." We surround this pan with a large exercise pen so that, during the early stages of labor, the bitch can move about the exercise area when not resting in the delivery pan and yet be confined to some extent. We can move in and out of the exercise pen to check the bitch's progress and to clean up as necessary.

Nursery setup: What has worked best in our kennel is the three-foot square metal whelping pen within its fencing. The level of the pan can be adjusted so that we can reach the puppies easily while sitting next to the pen. We place two of these pens side by side, with the small doorways open between the two. One is used as the nursery area, and the other is an easily cleaned exercise area for the bitch.

When the litter is old enough to start traveling around the pens, a small cardboard bridge can be placed between the two pens to prevent the puppies from catching a foot or slipping through the small gap between them.

Clean, cardboard panels attached to the periphery of the pens provide a well-insulated nursery, which is so important in maintaining the proper ambient temperature for the newborns.

In the most accessible corner of the nursery pen, place a heating pad *covered* with a piece of plywood. To afford traction for the puppies, a densely woven cloth can be applied to the plywood, and soft padding or newspaper can be used to cover the rest of the pen. The padding tends to cradle the developing bony parts. Pups and mother can move on or off the heated area as comfort dictates.

The nursery should be in a draft-free room, separate from the rest of the household. A heat lamp that can be adjusted as to height and direction placed over the whelping pen aids in maintaining a comfortably warm environment.

Labor

Introduce your bitch to her new quarters several days before her due date. If she has been in the kennel, bring her into the house and allow her to sleep in her "nursery."

Prediction of delivery: Most puppies come into the world between the fifty-ninth and seventieth day following breeding, sixty-three days being the average. Larger litters, as mentioned earlier, tend to be delivered earlier than smaller litters. In actuality, gestation lasts sixty days from fertilization. The actual day of fertilization is not easy to determine, unless you previously determined the onset of diestrus from serial vaginal smears.

Until recently, breeders relied on a drop in the bitch's rectal temperature to below 99 degrees as a sign that labor would follow within twenty-four hours. A sudden drop in progesterone blood level about twenty-four hours before delivery was considered to correspond with the temperature change. However, a study done by Vet Watch indicates that only 28 percent of bitches follow this pattern. Some never had a temperature drop, whereas others went into labor long after anticipated.

Labor, however, is precipitated by the sudden drop in the progesterone level in the blood.

Following serum progesterone levels is a much better predictor. With pregnancy progesterone, levels gradually increase to above 25 ng/ml, level off, and then drop to less than 2 ng/ml thirty-six to forty-eight hours before

Ch. Dismal Creek's Littl' Big Man, fifteen-inch dog (Ch. Page Mill Country Gentleman ex Ch. Dismal Creek's Splish Splash); multiple BIS, Group and Specialty winner; fifteen-inch NBC Beagle of the Year, 1992, 1993 and Beagle of the year, 1991. Owned by Mark Lister and Bruce Tague. *Cook*

Ch. Wishing Well's Love Song, fifteen-inch bitch (Ch. Lanbur Roshan Hi Fidelity ex Ch. Lanbur Love Notes). A Best in Specialty winner as well as a winner of the Award of Merit, NBC Specialty, 1994. Owned by Kathy Forbes and Patty A. Keenan. *Kohler*

whelping. For planned Caesarean sections, serial samples beginning four days before the first expected due date can pinpoint the safest time for the procedure, ensuring that the puppies have reached maximal intrauterine maturation.

A more sophisticated technique of monitoring labor and fetal heart rate— developed by Karen C. Snyder and Cheri C. Yoches at Vet Watch Corporation, Denver, Colorado—is available for rent. A sensor is strapped to the pregnant bitch's belly, which monitors the progress of labor as well as fetal heart rate every twelve hours or more often as indicated with a hookup by phone to the company's computer. A simultaneous verbal report goes to the bitch's owner. Abnormal labor patterns and failing fetal heart rate alert the owner and veterinarian to trouble. A significant drop in newborn mortality rate from 33 percent to 6 percent has been achieved with this diagnostic tool.

For those breeders who choose not to or cannot use these diagnostic aids, the traditional taking of the bitch's rectal temperature three times a day can be useful. But remember that not all dams follow the expected pattern. You will need to watch it closely for signs of impending labor.

The first stage of labor (as the cervix dilates) is marked by frequent urination and sometimes refusal of food. Labor progresses with the bitch showing periodic restlessness alternating with nesting, panting and obvious discomfort. A mucous discharge is normal.

Once the cervix is completely dilated, obvious uterine contractions are palpable, and the bitch begins to bear down, groaning as she does. Vomiting and frequent urination may occur during this stage as well.

If no active labor follows within twenty-four hours after the temperature/progesterone level drops, notify your veterinarian. A greenish-black discharge indicates placental separation and signals an obstetrical emergency.

Delivery

The bitch's perineum bulges as the puppy makes its way through the pelvic outlet into the vaginal canal. A sac containing amniotic fluid usually precedes the puppy appearing at the vulva. If this sac ruptures too early, a dry birth may result. Once the puppy has made its way into the vaginal canal, pup and placenta usually deliver with three to five good contractions. If progress is slow, *feathering*—stroking the anterior wall of the vagina with your gloved forefinger—may facilitate better contractions. Placentas don't always arrive with the puppy, so make sure that all are accounted for.

Puppies present head first about equally as hindfeet first. Because the head is more compact and firmer in consistency, it acts as a better dilator of the birth canal than the feet in a footling or breech birth presentation.

If no puppy delivers within thirty minutes, an obstetrical emergency is declared, and a Caesarean section should be considered. Time lost in transit to the veterinary hospital lessens the chances of that puppy's survival. This is especially true if the first puppy is a footling.

The intervals between deliveries vary from minutes to several hours. If six hours elapse without any sign of labor between puppies, notify your veterinarian.

Most Beagle bitches will immediately clean off the sac that surrounds the puppy at birth and bite the umbilical cord through. Watch that the cord is not bitten off too close to the puppy's abdominal wall. The dam's enthusiastic and vigorous licking and shoving around of the pup stimulate the newborn, forcing liquid from its lungs and helping clear the airway.

If the bitch does not begin to take care of the puppy immediately or appears too rough, remove the puppy and placenta from the whelping box, place it in a clean towel and quickly wipe away all membranes from the mouth and nose. Briskly rub the puppy, holding it with its head down. Gentle aspiration of fluid from nose and mouth with a soft rubber bulb syringe helps clear the airway. Don't be concerned about separating pup from placenta until after the airway is clear and the pup is breathing well. The way to check for good circulation is to check for pink foot pads, abdomen and nose leather. Crying facilitates lung expansion; snapping toes and feet stimulates crying. Hold the head and body firmly with both hands so that the head and neck are splinted, and then bring your hands down from above your head to in front of you with a quick movement. This also helps to clear fluid from the puppy's airway.

Once the puppy is breathing and its tummy is pink, clamp the umbilical cord with a hemostat about three-quarters inch from the abdomen and tear the cord with your fingernails on the placental side of the clamp. Clamping and tearing aid in sealing of the cord, whereas cutting with scissors allows seepage of blood from the puppy and may provide an opportunity for infection.

Check each puppy for any abnormalities, such as cleft palate or defects in the abdominal wall. Record the weight and description of each puppy.

At this point, return the puppy to its mother for more stimulation and licking, unless the mother is already engaged in delivering her next offspring. The additional attention from the bitch helps to clear the airway further but also aids in evacuation of the sticky meconium—the first stool passed by the newborn. Vigorous newborns gravitate quickly to the nipple for suckling, which in turn stimulates the onset of the next sequence of labor.

All placentas should be accounted for. Bitches, if allowed, will eat them, and vomiting may then follow. Certainly, it is nature's way of cleaning up the birthing area and giving nourishment to the bitch. It is the breeder's choice as to how many placentas are consumed. Probably one is enough!

If delivery is a long, drawn-out process, you can offer the bitch water and/or warm chicken or beef broth.

When the last of the pups has arrived, wash the blood and fluid off the dam and dry her thoroughly. The simplest way is to put her in a bathtub and wash her hindquarters under warm, running water. Rinse all soap off, and dry the dam thoroughly. The dam and her pups are then moved into the permanent nursery. Adjust the heat lamp as needed to provide a warm environment. A relaxed bitch settles down with her brood and ultimately sleeps.

At this point, you can, too!

Unfortunately, some Beagle dams, especially with their first litters, are nervous and need to be carefully monitored initially. Some are uncaring as to where they lie down, and newborns may have to be moved quickly to avoid suffocation under the dam. This is especially a worry with bitches that have had a Caesarean section. Often, they are still sedated and disoriented from the anesthetic, even though they are awake and on their feet. These bitches are better off crated, separated from their litters, except when the breeder is present and supervising nursing every hour or two.

Once the bitch recovers totally from her anesthetic, she may need a day or two before her milk is adequate and before she is comfortable with her pups. The pups need supplemental feeding and even more careful supervision. Some dams will nurse their puppies happily but most fastidiously will absolutely refuse to clean up after them. These pups will need regular stimulation following nursing to induce defecation and urination for the first week or ten days.

Make sure that nursing puppies know how to "latch on" to the teats and that they have a good sucking reflex. A vigorous sucking reflex will be apparent if you insert your little finger into the pup's mouth; the suction of a eager puppy is unmistakable. If the puppy rejects the finger or simply gums it, the pup may need to be warmed up and carefully observed.

Many veterinarians recommend that the dam be injected with oxytocin following the completion of delivery. This stimulates contraction of the uterus, which aids in evacuating any remaining fluid and tissues within the uterus as well as stimulating milk production. *Follow your veterinarian's advice on this.*

Caesarean Section

Caesarean sections are not uncommon with Beagle bitches, especially with the thirteen-inch variety. Whether done as an emergency intervention during labor or by plan, it is important that the veterinarian be experienced. It may take some looking to find one who enjoys working with breeders and fits your needs.

Beagle Puppies—And the Best Shot at Survival

NORMAL BEAGLE PUPPIES

At birth, as with other canines, Beagle puppies are born with sealed eyelids and poor hearing, if any. Ears are mere tabs. There is some reaction on the part of the puppies to odors, pain, touch and temperature change. The puppy will quite promptly seek its dam by crawling and showing poor muscular coordination with its head flopping or swinging from side to side. It is capable of righting itself and will show frequent muscle twitches or involuntary contractions while sleeping.

Crying occurs when it is separated from its mother, if hungry, chilled or in pain. Ninety percent of its time is spent sleeping. Normal urination and defecation occur only with stimulation. Umbilical cords dry up and drop off at two or three days.

Beagle newborns are black and white or pale tan and white. A puppy that may appear white at birth will be a pale tan and white as an adult. Pups that carry the lemon factor frequently have a brownish cast to the black portion of their coats, a cast that fades out as the puppies grow.

Normal Development

Eyes open: 10 to 14 days, but can be as late as 21 days.

Ears open: 13 to 17 days.

Begins walking: About 18 days.

Urinates/defecates without assistance: 3 to 4 weeks.

First teeth: Usually about 3 weeks.

Primary socialization: 3 to 10 weeks is the most crucial period.

113

Permanent teeth: Beginning at about 16 weeks, completed by six months.

Sexual maturity: From 8 months to 18 months. Some bitches, however, do not have their first season until age 24 months.

The period from ten weeks to six to eight months (about puberty) sees continuing growth, independence and roaming behavior if the Beagle is allowed to do so. Mounting behavior in both male and female occurs, and the male begins to hike his hindleg to urinate instead of squatting.

In Beagles, "adolescence" lasts from about six months to twenty-four months and is marked by playfulness, chewing, digging and progressively greater exercise requirements.

By two years, having achieved adulthood (questionable in some instances!), most Beagles will spend much of the midday sleeping with periods of activity in the morning and late afternoon.

Weaning

At about three weeks of age, normal Beagle puppies may be started on a warm, mushy gruel of commercial simulated bitch's milk, strained chicken and rice or Hi-Pro baby cereal. Orphan pups can be started earlier with baby cereal and simulated bitch's milk. We have found that puppies do not gain as well on a diet consisting only of the milk product and that they are always hungry.

Offer the meals in a raised pan, encouraging each pup to lap or lick food from your fingers at first. Gradually increase the number of meals offered per day to four or five over the following three or four weeks. Offer the meals after the dam has been separated from the babies for a while so that they are hungry when you do so.

Bottled water should be available from about three weeks on; make sure that the container is not so large that the puppies may fall into it and be unable to get out.

Often, the pups will flock about the dam's food dish as she eats, occasionally prompting a disgruntled response from mother. Of course, the dam, in turn, is more than happy to polish off any of the pups' leavings.

The puppies' food mixture should be gradually changed to include a good grade of commercial dry puppy food, reduced to fine granules in the food processor. Cottage cheese, baby chicken/beef and yogurt can be added for flavor. Vitamins can be added to the food as soon as the puppies are eating. Careful dosages are required, because commercial dog foods contain added vitamins and minerals.

Between six and eight weeks, most Beagle dams will begin to discourage nursing, becoming restless and irritable because the pups' sharp teeth hurt.

Separating the bitch from the pups during the day and returning it to them for the night for the final few days before total separation makes for a gradual break rather than a "cold turkey" break.

Occasionally, especially with a singleton puppy, the bitch is content to remain forever with her get. Actually, this works well for the solitary puppy, which then has companionship, a playmate and a teacher.

Once the pups are on solid food, they should be tested for heartworm, and a preventative can be administered.

Don't be surprised if the pups prefer nursing to "dining out" at first. Ultimately, they will learn. After all, have you ever seen a healthy adult Beagle that won't wolf down whatever is placed in front of it?

The singleton puppy, without the competitive pushing and shoving of siblings "at the trough," may be slower to learn to eat. Placing the food pan on the floor and sticking your own head down to it and making slurping noises as though you are enjoying this marvelous feast may encourage the puppy to join in.

Immunizations

By the time this book is available to Beaglers, new information about the most current, safest and best schedule of immunizations is likely to be available. Infectious diseases to which dogs are susceptible and for which vaccinations are available include distemper, hepatitis, parainfluenza, leptospirosis, parvovirus, corona virus, bordetella and rabies.

Immunity: Newborn Beagles acquire passive immunity via the dam's first milk (colostrum) during the first twenty-four to thirty-six hours of life. Because the amount of circulating antibodies in the mother's blood varies, it is difficult to know when the passive immunity of the pups begins to drop. Since circulating antibodies in the pup may block the development of active immunity with premature vaccinations, most immunization programs rely on a series of injections. This increases the chance that one or more of the injections will be of optimal timing.

Schedule: You and your veterinarian can work out an appropriate schedule. Recently, there has been some suggestive evidence that early vaccination with AdenoVirus 2 prior to fourteen weeks may lower resistance to parvovirus infections. At-risk kennels (those with a history of recurring parvovirus infections) may require a special program of vaccinations.

Once the initial vaccinations are completed, annual boosters are necessary. Rabies vaccination frequency varies with your home-state regulations.

In the instance of orphaned puppies that do not receive the dam's colostrum within that first time period, transfusion of dog plasma from healthy dogs may be an aid to early protection. Hemopet, a service developed by W. Jean Dodds, DVM, offers such a preparation, in addition to whole blood products, in the Southern California area. Those living in other areas should rely on their veterinarian's advice or seek out a large veterinary hospital, possibly attached to a veterinary school.

Feeding Schedule

As puppies reach six or seven weeks of age, it is good to feed them individually, since the pups will probably eat at different rates, and the "piggy" ones will get the lion's share. By feeding them separately, you can titre the amounts to the puppies' individual needs. Placing each puppy in a crate adjacent to or facing each other stimulates their competition for food.

Three to four meals a day consisting of a good grade of dry commercial puppy-growth kibble, flavored with baby chicken or beef, cottage cheese, yogurt or egg yolk, works best for the six- to twelve-week puppies. Supply a bowl of condensed milk (1:1 dilution) at night as well as some dry puppy kibble for overnight nibbling. This nocturnal meal can be dropped by twelve weeks.

At sixteen weeks, meals can be decreased to two, but the quantity of each should be proportionately increased. Weight should be watched. Begin a good vitamin/mineral supplement and heartworm preventative as soon as the puppy is eating well.

Full growth occurs sometime between eight and twelve months. At this point, a maintenance dry food should be substituted for the growth formula, and one meal a day is offered. Small amounts of meat, cottage cheese, yogurt or acidophilus milk will add animal protein. One meal a day works well until the Beagle begins to age, when two smaller meals per day place a lesser demand on the heart and circulatory system.

Dewclaws

All Beagle pups are born with anterior dewclaws and some with rear ones as well. If the condition of the newborn warrants, the dewclaws can be removed at three days of age.

Rear dewclaws generally are large and unsightly; anteriors are smaller and easier to remove. It is a painful procedure for the puppy, unfortunately, and not every breeder has the stomach for this home surgery. Either you or your veterinarian can do it. Sometimes, the trip to the veterinarian and the separation from the dam add even more stress to the pups.

The amputation site must be watched over several days for any signs of infection. Usually, the little crust or scab that forms drops off after two or three days, and the area heals quickly.

ENSURING PUPPY SURVIVAL

The three most important factors in newborn survival are air, heat and hydration. *Never forget these.*

Normal Beagle puppies range in weight from eight ounces to as much as fifteen ounces. The average is probably about ten ounces. In our kennel, any puppy less than eight ounces is considered to be more at risk, and at the first sign of any problem, treatment is immediate. Normal Beagle newborns have pink tummies and foot pads; they are active and suckle enthusiastically. A footling at birth may have a dusky tinge to its hindfeet for the first twenty-four hours. Bladder and bowel function occur only with stimulation, either by the mother's licking or by gently tapping the pup's bottom with a moist tissue or cotton ball. Don't rub, because it may irritate these tender parts.

Any alteration from normal newborn behavior can be critical to survival, and early and proper remedies should be instituted at the first sign of any problem.

Air

Fully expanded lungs and a clear airway are essential to a puppy's survival. After you have done everything to ensure this, the newborns should be watched for respiratory difficulties and pale skin pigment.

Listen to the puppies' chests twenty-four hours after birth. A stethoscope, reasonable in price, is a worthwhile investment under any circumstances. But, even without the help of a stethoscope, you can simply place the puppy up to your ear and listen for any "rattles" during respiration. Normally, respiratory rate can vary between fifteen and thirty-five breaths per minute. If the puppy sounds *wet*, an incubator with an oxygen supply can be lifesaving.

"Celeste" with her two-day-old litter. Photo shows a whelping box constructed with a "pig rail" to prevent the dam from lying on her pups and a thermometer to monitor the temperature. The heat lamp above the box is raised and lowered to maintain the correct temperature. *Kristine Kraeuter*

Strapping the puppy to a small board with its head dependent about thirty degrees simulates crying and drainage, which are both essential to clearing the lungs.

Pneumonia in a newborn is usually a lethal disease.

Heat

A puppy's rectal temperature just following delivery is 101° Fahrenheit. This quickly drops with an ambient temperature of 70° Fahrenheit. Since that is the average room temperature comfortable for humans, it is essential that additional heat sources be supplied to newborns.

A warm room, padded hot water bottles, an adjustable heat lamp at some distance and a heating pad, if used cautiously, are all options. Most essential is a maternally-inclined bitch with well-developed mammary tissue to provide the external temperature needed to maintain a normal 96° Fahrenheit rectal temperature in the newborn.

Temperature-control mechanisms are poorly developed in newborns, so minor alterations in any heating device will adversely affect the smaller and weaker pups especially. After one week of age, normal puppy temperature is 99° Fahrenheit as a result of more efficient development of the normal temperature-regulating system. The well-known phenomenon of maternal rejection is most likely due to the puppy being cooler than normal. And, of course, that is the puppy that most needs to be close to its siblings and its mother's belly. Sometimes, warming that puppy may reverse the bitch's rejection.

You do not need to perform a routine check of the rectal temperature of the older newborns unless a problem exists.

Signs of chilling are crying, increased restlessness and movement of the head from side to side as the pup seeks a heat source. Poor mammary development leads to easy chilling, because there is less than optimal breast tissue to act as a radiator. Attempts to feed a puppy when it is chilled are useless, because the milk substitute simply pools in the stomach and does not move on into the intestine. *A puppy must be warmed before it is fed.* Eventually, if the pup's temperature drops below 94° Farhenheit, paralysis of the bowel occurs; the respiratory rate drops, and there is a concomitant decrease in immunity. These pups are extremely susceptible to infection.

The best way to warm a chilled puppy is a gradual one that combines an outside heat source with stimulation of the newborn. Place the pup in your coat pocket or under your clothes next to your skin so that your body heat warms it slowly. Your activity will passively keep the puppy moving. Placing a chilled puppy directly under a heat lamp simply dehydrates it, adding to the problems.

Another helpful technique is to place the chilled pup in a separate small, toweled box with a sealable plastic food bag or plastic glove containing warm (not too hot) water.

Once the puppy is warm and active again, other measures can be taken as needed, such as supplemental feeding.

Gradually, as the puppy matures, its ability to regulate its own temperature develops. But outside sources of heat should be available as indicated.

Hydration

Newborns are 82 percent water at birth, dropping to 68 percent after five months of age. Water is the essential requirement in the first few hours of life. Although you might have heard that newborns can go twelve hours without nourishment, our experience differs. Beagle pups that are slow to suckle during the first six to eight hours need supplementation. Dehydration can occur far too quickly.

A dehydrated Beagle puppy is limp, less active, loses its sucking reflex and rapidly loses body heat. Gently pinch and lift the skin on the back of the pup's neck. When released, a hydrated puppy's skin returns to its normal position almost immediately, whereas the dried-out pup's remains tented. *Immediate hydration is required under such circumstances.*

Dehydration is usually accompanied by hypothermia (lowered body temperature) and hypoglycemia (low blood sugar), so the total symptom complex must be treated. The gastrointestinal tract will not be able to process a milk substitute by mouth, causing further problems.

The puppy should be warmed and initially given a *subcutaneous* (under the skin) injection of a warmed solution of one part Ringer's lactate to one part 5 percent glucose. Your veterinarian can provide you with a 250 cubic centimeter (cc) plastic container of the solution. It is a simple matter to withdraw a few cubic centimeters at a time and inject the solution with a hypodermic needle.

Technique: Clean the skin over the shoulder on one side with alcohol. Then insert the sterile needle, size twenty-four or twenty-five, which is attached to the syringe containing the solution, just under the skin. Draw back on the plunger to make sure the needle is not in a blood vessel, and then slowly inject the solution. Jacob Mosier, DVM, recommends one cc per ounce of body weight of 5 percent to 10 percent dextrose, which can be obtained from your veterinarian, followed by tube feeding after the puppy is warmed and better hydrated. His formula is 0.25 cc/ounce body weight at fifteen- to thirty-minute intervals until the puppy is well hydrated and urinating.

We have found in the moderately dehydrated pup that 2 to 3 ccs of the Ringer's lactate with 5 percent glucose, administered subcutaneously and repeated in one hour to the opposite shoulder results in an almost miraculous return of vigor, activity, hunger and a good sucking reflex. At this point, the puppy is ready to nurse.

Some Beagle pups that weigh less than seven ounces at birth are slower to come along. If not encouraged and supplemented promptly so that

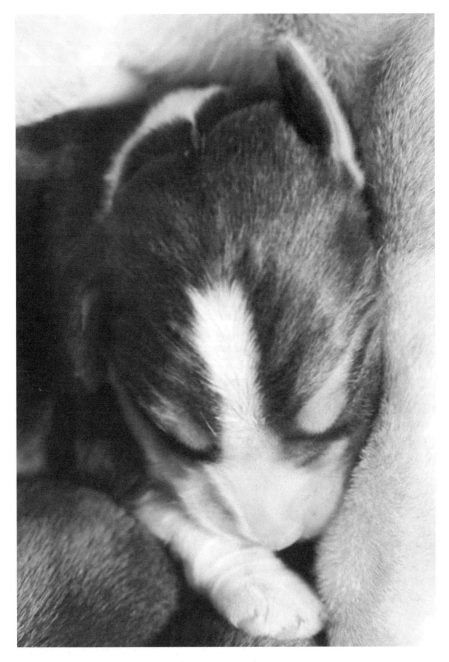

One-day-old puppy by Echo Run Peacemaker ex Ch. Beamer's Just The Wright Touch.
Julie Wright

"Elsie," a Brushy Run puppy, at two-and-one-half weeks, is comfortable on the scale. *Kristine Kraeuter*

normal weight gain occurs, these pups are more vulnerable to dehydration and infection.

Weighing

The best monitor of puppy health is a gradual and steady weight gain. Because newborns can fade so quickly, it is important not only to observe and feel pups frequently, but to weigh them twice daily for the first three weeks. Once daily is sufficient from three to six weeks. Weekly weights from then until sixteen weeks can furnish a good guideline for estimating eventual adult size.

Healthy pups double their birth weight in seven to ten days and triple it in two weeks. A very slight weight loss in the first twenty-four hours, less than 10 percent total body weight, may occur in some pups, followed by a steady gain. A weight loss of more than 10 percent requires immediate supplementation. In practice, we supplement if the pup has not gained within the first twenty-four hours.

Ten-day-old puppies nursing vigorously. *Lynne Heltne*

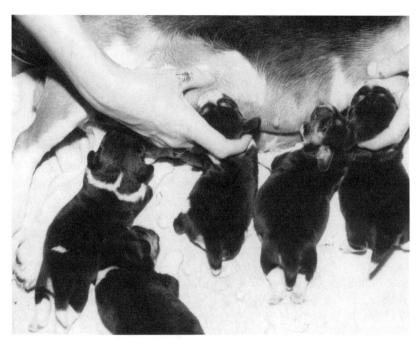

This picture of a one-week-old litter shows how to assist weaker pups by supporting them at the nipple and massaging the breast with fingers to increase milk flow. *Lynne Heltne*

Nursing

Sucking ability varies in Beagle babies. Most "latch on" immediately, pumping away with the front feet, and are able to withstand some competition for teats from other siblings. There are some, however, who are inefficient sucklers. These make a great to-do over the nipple, smacking and nuzzling and appearing to be nursing well. Not so. Tummies may feel and look full, but it is just swallowed saliva and air, not milk. Check the sucking reflex by inserting your little finger in the pup's mouth to see how tightly it wraps its tongue around it and how strongly it pulls. When latched on to the nipple, a good nurser will maintain strong contractions of the jaw muscles, which can be easily felt by placing thumb and forefinger on either side of the pup's muzzle.

The size and shape of the dam's nipples play an important part in the efficiency of nursing. The bitches of some lines have small, flattened nipples. Pups from these bitches may need extra help in getting latched on initially until the nipples develop more shape. The two breasts closest to the hind legs seem to regularly become impacted with milk, and it is important that the puppies use all the nipples. Individual pups vary in their preferences, and occasionally a pup may nurse only from a favorite nipple. Small puppies can be easily pushed aside by larger, stronger ones, so it is important to observe pups and dam frequently, giving any assistance needed.

Supplementation

Newborns require ten to seventy calories per pound per day for the first week of life. Caloric requirements increase to seventy to eighty calories per pound per day by the second week, eighty to ninety calories per pound per day by the third week and ninety to 100 calories per pound per day by the fourth week. Frequent, small feedings every two hours enable the pup to handle the volume required without overloading its digestive tract.

Bitch's milk substitutes, Esbilac™ and Nurturall™ are easily obtained. The latter, less likely to cause diarrhea, has the advantage of a longer refrigerator life. An every-two-hour schedule is easier on the puppy than the three to four times a day recommended by the manufacturer. We dilute the formula to two parts distilled water to one part formula for the first twenty-four to forty-eight hours of life. Concentration can then be gradually increased to full strength by the fourth day of life. Overloading the digestive tract can be fatal, as we have sadly discovered.

Newborns do not develop a gag reflex until about nine days of age. Therefore, one has to be careful how the puppy is fed.

If its sucking reflex is strong and the reason for supplementation is a bitch whose milk output is inadequate, bottle feeding works well. A pet nurser or a baby bottle with a preemie nipple does the trick. Using a twenty-one-gauge needle that has been flame-sterilized, poke two holes in the nipple to allow adequate flow.

A post-Caesarean section dam getting some help with her new pups. *Robin Whitelock*

With a weakened puppy, tube feeding provides the safest method. For an eight-ounce puppy, a #8 French catheter/feeding tube of soft, flexible material fitted on a 10 cc syringe will be appropriate for the size of the esophagus. For a one-pound puppy (sometimes you do get one!), a #16 French catheter is the correct size.

Technique: While holding the puppy upright, measure the distance from the mouth to the end of the last rib, and mark the feeding tube. Slide the tube to the back of the pup's mouth, and it will start to swallow the tube. If the newborn coughs, remove the tube and begin again. *Always check to make sure the tube is in the stomach, not the trachea (windpipe)*. The airway is clear if the puppy cries when its toes are pinched. Slowly syringe the warmed formula through the tube after eliminating any air from the syringe. While feeding, always hold the puppy upright to facilitate the flow of the formula.

Always burp the puppy following each feeding by either rubbing the tummy or gently stroking the sides of the abdomen in a downward direction. Frequently, burping occurs while you are stimulating the anogenital area to induce urination and defecation.

COMMON PROBLEMS IN NEWBORNS

Fading Puppy Syndrome

Characteristically, the fading puppy is in the smaller birth weight range. Though vigorous and seemingly normal immediately after birth, it is slower to gain, if at all, during the first twenty-four to forty-eight hours. It may begin to sleep more, miss a nursing or two, and have semiliquid or liquid stools. This syndrome may be present in a number of potentially serious problems, but usually it is simply a matter of a small, less-prepared puppy that has to be helped along.

Warming, subcutaneous fluids, if necessary, and 1 cc to 2 ccs of 5 percent glucose or dextrose administered by mouth every twenty minutes initially, increased to 5 ccs to 6 ccs about thirty to sixty minutes apart, will usually restore the puppy almost magically.

Diarrhea or liquid stools in the newborn simply means the pH of the digestive tract is acidic. A half-dropperful of milk of magnesia will alkalinize the gut.

Once the puppy has good color, is vigorous and its sucking reflex is present, it can be placed back with its mother. Most likely, supplemental feedings of diluted simulated bitch's milk several times plus frequent assists at the nipple will be needed. Usually, with this help over the first four days, the tiny puppy is over the worst of it.

Diarrhea

Normal puppy stools, after the initial dark, sticky meconium is passed, are yellow and soft but formed.

One of England's top-winning Beagles during the 1970s and early 1980s is Ch. Beacott Buckthorn, shown at age twelve and one-half years. First in the Hound Group at Crufts, 1981, as well as BIS at several Championship shows, he is owned by Sylvia and Phillip Tutchener.

Diarrhea can range from simply a softer, more frequent stool with small curds of undigested milk to a profuse yellow liquid.

The former type of diarrhea is most common and fortunately poses no danger to the puppy. Causes include too hearty nursing, mixture of formula fed (as when supplementation is given along with nursing) or simply acidification of the digestive tract for whatever reason.

Symptomatic treatment consists of one-half dropperful of Kaopectate™ four times a day for an eight-ounce puppy and one dropperful for a fourteen- to sixteen-ouncer. If the stools are very frequent, Kaopectate™ can be given after each bowel movement until frequency decreases. Antibiotics are seldom needed. Most of these puppies continue to suckle well and gain weight despite the diarrhea.

However, if the diarrhea is profuse, dehydration can occur rapidly. In this instance, placing the puppy on subcutaneous fluids, as described earlier, and resting the intestinal tract for twenty-four hours will often handle the situation. Alternatively, dextrose and water or Pedialyte™ (an over-the-counter pediatric preparation for babies with diarrhea) by mouth will keep the puppy hydrated. Of course, your veterinarian should be consulted.

Some breeders report that a continuing mild diarrhea, resisting all efforts at treatment, subsides only when soft solid foods are begun.

Swollen Eyes

In spite of your best efforts to maintain a clean environment for the puppies, the possibility of contamination is always there. If an infectious agent enters the closed eyes of the newborn, a swollen-appearing eye results. Pus accumulates between the eyelid and the orb. The puppy then looks like the magnified head of a fly with a bulge behind the sealed lids.

Prompt treatment is mandatory, because a generalized infection of the eyeball can result. Treatment includes application of hot compresses, gently prying the lids open and expressing pus several times a day along with insertion of an antibiotic ophthalmic ointment four times a day. However, consult your veterinarian just to be safe.

These puppies, on rare occasions, will develop a dry-eye syndrome (q.v.). So watch carefully once the eyes are open. Check to see that the eyeball is glistening and well-lubricated. Any discharge or squinting developing later requires immediate veterinary attention. The eventual onset of dry eye may indicate a preexisting vulnerability that resulted in the early infection.

Slow to Walk

It is not uncommon for one puppy in a Beagle litter to be slower to stand and walk than its siblings. The rear legs seem to be weaker, usually extended behind the torso, and the puppy spends most of the time on its belly. It scoots itself around primarily by pulling with the forelegs. When this condition is associated with a flat chest, front to back, and extended forelegs as well, the puppy is known as a "swimmer."

Once it is clear that the pup cannot get its hind legs under itself, you can support the puppy with your hand and encourage the use of its limbs. Some breeders report excellent results with vitamin E injections. Bob and Louise Merrill of Starcrest Beagles built a clever U-shaped "walking trough," just wide enough to support the sides of the puppy. The afflicted pup walks from one end to the other at regular intervals throughout the day. The pups love it.

"Supported swimming" in a small tub of water also provides exercise for the limbs without requiring the puppy to support itself by standing.

For the "swimmer" whose front legs are also extended, hobbling the legs with a figure-eight bandage brings the legs under the body with enough room for walking.

Optimal protection for soft chests and sliding feet is afforded by well-padded bedding with a surface that provides good traction. Frequent turning of the pup that lies on its tummy all the time helps distribute the weight evenly over the rib cage. Happily, affected puppies usually outgrow the condition.

Am. & Can. Ch. Lenergie Clancy Lower The Boom, fifteen-inch dog, (Ch. Pinedell's Clancy ex Lanbur Plaid Patches) owned by Bill and Sue Gear. A BIS winner in Canada and multiple Group winner in the United States. Best of Breed at the NBC Specialty, 1992. *Alex Smith*

Worm Infestation

Roundworm infestation is very common. Encysted larvae in the dam reactivated by pregnancy pass through the placenta to the puppies. Early worming at three to four weeks is indicated. Safe preparations, such as piperazine or Nemex™, are given at weekly intervals until the stools are clear. Reworming four weeks later should suffice, unless reinfestation occurs; Interceptor™ can be given at about eight weeks of age if necessary. Always follow the recommendations of your veterinarian regarding worming.

In parts of the United States where hookworm is common, an infested dam passes larvae though both the placenta and her milk. Hookworm infestation is particularly dangerous to newborns and must be treated as early as two to four weeks, if necessary. Your veterinarian must supervise treatment.

UNCOMMON PROBLEMS IN NEWBORNS

Septicemia

This generalized blood-borne infection may occur at anywhere from one to forty days of age. Most common infectious organisms are *E. coli*, beta-hemolytic streptococcus and staphylococcus. The most common source of the infection is an undiagnosed chronic metritis (infection of the uterus) in the dam, but it can also arise in an infected breast.

In addition to the typical fading-puppy syndrome, these pups will deteriorate rapidly. They will evidence crying, increased respiratory rate, bloating and, finally, shock and death. One after another of the pups in the litter dies.

Good prenatal management of the bitch, as described earlier, is mandatory. Treatment of the affected pups includes separation from the bitch, fluids, warming and antibiotics. Many of the antibiotics that are effective in adults are not in newborns, so careful selection must be made.

All dead puppies should be autopsied and histological studies done. A culture of blood drawn from the heart shortly after death is essential.

Reports from our current conformation population indicate an occasional outbreak in a few kennels. During the 1970s, however, the incidence was quite high, with some breeders losing litter after litter until appropriate antibiotic treatment of the bitches was initiated. With the current veterinary knowledge and practice, the incidence has dropped dramatically.

Canine Herpes Virus

Infection by a herpes-like virus (CHV) occurs in pups *less than three weeks of age only*. A soft, greenish-yellow stool is the first sign, followed by persistent, painful crying. Death can occur within twelve to twenty-four hours.

Puppies acquire the virus via the infected genital tract of the bitch.

Treatment consists of fluids to relieve dehydration and low blood sugar, antibiotics and raising the ambient temperature to 100° Fahrenheit for three hours and then dropping it to 93 to 95° Fahrenheit for the rest of a twenty-four-hour period. Rectal temperature of the puppy must be maintained above 96.8° Fahrenheit, because the virus cannot multiply above that temperature. Serum from a bitch that has previously lost litters due to CHV given to the afflicted puppies provides antibodies to the virus. Persistently crying pups have suffered profound liver damage and should be put down. Those pups that are not yet crying can be saved with immediate treatment.

Those carrier bitches that develop antibodies to CHV pass those antibodies on to puppies in subsequent litters, but not all bitches do so. Therefore, further breedings of these bitches must be weighed carefully.

Fortunately, reports of CHV in our current conformation population have been rare.

Toxic Milk Syndrome

Characterized by diarrhea, bloating and a red, swollen anus, toxic milk syndrome affects the entire litter.

Though the bitch appears perfectly healthy, her uterus has not involuted (shrunken down) properly following delivery. Toxic protein breakdown in the accumulated fluid is passed in the milk to the puppies.

Remove these pups from the dam for twenty-four to forty-eight hours and treat with oral glucose and water only. Treatment of the dam consists of ergotamine to flush out the uterus and antibiotics plus some steroid. After twenty-four to forty-eight hours, the pups can be returned to the dam.

Hydrocephalus

Excessive accumulation of fluid in the ventricles (cavities) of the brain produces puppies that fail to thrive and have difficulty with coordination, and it is frequently accompanied by a persistently open *fontanelle*, the central "soft spot" at the top of the skull.

One form is certainly genetic, but other possible causes include nutritional deficiencies in the dam during pregnancy and a high concentration of nitrates in the bitch's drinking water.

Scattered reports of an occasional hydrocephalic Beagle puppy in a litter have been made over the past twenty to thirty years. Pedigrees of three Beagle litters, each with two hydrocephalic puppies, strongly suggest a genetic basis.

Kidney Disease

Though deaths from kidney disease in Beagle puppies have been reported from time to time in our current population, the causes of the kidney problem have varied.

Symptoms generally include failure to thrive and excessive urination and water intake.

The information available to date suggests that these problems are more likely due to some congenital malformation, produced during fetal development in the uterus, instead of genetic.

An appealing litter of eight Starcrest puppies at four weeks.

Ch. Someday's Practically Perfect, thirteen-inch bitch (Ch. Whiskey Creek's Headliner ex Ch. Someday's Pretty Woman), owned by Dr. and Mrs. John R. Frazier, shown winning Best in Sweepstakes, NBC Specialty, 1995, at six and one-half months under breeder-judge Eddie Dzuik. *Tom di Giacomo*

Skyline's Play The Game, fifteen-inch dog (Ch. Tashwould Final Warning ex Ch. Wishing Well's Love Song), sixteen-month-old puppy, owned by Kathy A. Forbes and Wishing Well Kennels, Reg.

Sorting Your Puppies

Sorting your Beagle pups into show prospects and quality pets is generally not difficult in a tightly linebred litter. What is difficult, however, is evaluating a first-time outcross or distantly linebred litter. Unfortunately, in most cases, early decisions must be made to ensure the best timing for placement of puppies in their new homes.

HOW DO MY PUPPIES GROW?

Most Beagle puppies look just great at six weeks, but by eight weeks changes begin to occur. Muzzles may narrow, front legs may curve and rears look pinched. Obviously, these pups fall into the pet category. By twelve weeks, the puppy is virtually a miniature of the adult dog. This is the time to finalize your sorting.

Judge each pup in a show stack and on a lead in motion, grading against the Standard. The well-known breeders Arthur and Carroll Gordon (Page Mill Beagles) evaluated each pup by the Beagle point scale. Those pups scoring more than 90 were considered to be show prospects.

A soft topline at twelve weeks is a soft topline forever. Adult balance depends on the particular Beagle line. In ours, a short-on-leg twelve-week-old will be a short-on-leg adult. We have watched pups from other lines produce good-sized fifteen-inch dogs that appear short-legged at twelve weeks but grow to be well-balanced adults. So you must know how the various lines of Beagles develop.

From twelve weeks to six months of age, the Beagle puppy grows in "fits and starts" in most cases. Heads change from proper to narrow "shoeboxes." Rears may grow faster than fronts in height. Pups lengthen before gaining height. Spindly tails gain brush.

Some pups grow proportionately. In our experience, the pup that does so, always maintaining its balance, usually falls into the thirteen-inch variety as an adult.

Basic skeletal structure does not change; a good shoulder is a good shoulder regardless of age. But movement may vary because of erratic growth until adulthood or maturity is reached.

Most thirteen-inch bitches reach full growth by about eight months of age; thirteen-inch males may grow for a bit longer. Fifteens keep on growing until about twelve months of age.

PREDICTION OF SIZE

Accurate prediction of adult height at the shoulders is impossible!

Accepting that fact, there are some general factors that can help you make an "educated" guess about which variety a hound is more likely to grow into. Each closely bred Beagle line has its own growth patterns. Jean Dills (Pickadilly Beagles) uses multiple measurements, including height, hock length and circumference of legs at six weeks as indicators. Others use the puppy's weight at four weeks by which to project the correct adult variety.

In our closely linebred stock, weights of all puppies were recorded at four, six, eight, twelve, sixteen weeks and at five and six months. We found that there was a borderline region in which either thirteen-inch or small fifteen-inch varieties can lie, obvious when graphing the data. The weight at twelve weeks is suggestive of adult size, but not certain. Additional weights at later ages may make more accurate prediction possible.

Obviously, figures from one family cannot be directly applied to another. But perhaps the general principle can be used. Remember that weights must be taken on the *same* scale. Even then, it is virtually impossible to obtain totally accurate figures, because puppies wiggle around along with the weight indicator.

Parents of either variety can and do produce get of either variety.

It is wise to alert prospective buyers that final size of a growing puppy cannot be guaranteed!

BITES

Evaluating bites in your young Beagle puppies can be a tricky business. What you see today may change over a period of months.

Overshot Bites

A severely overshot mouth may be obvious shortly after birth or, for that matter, at birth. The puppy appears chinless. When viewed from underneath, a small portion of the roof of the mouth (the hard palate) may be seen, even with the mouth closed. These pups may have difficulty nursing.

Ch. Just-Wright Swashbuckler at three-and-one-half months, owned by Julie Wright.

Ch. Just-Wright Swashbuckler, fifteen-inch dog (Ch. Just-Wright Lethal Weapon ex Ch. Just-Wright She's Like The Wind), owned by Jo-Ann and Roy Kusumoto and Julie Wright, grew up to become a multiple Group winner.

The less severely overshot mouth may not be obvious until the baby teeth appear. There has been at least one instance of an overshot bite showing up as late as seven or eight months of age. Whether this condition will correct with full growth is uncertain. Personally, we have yet to see an overbite that is apparent early in life correct itself as the Beagle matures.

Undershot Bites

Like overshot mouths, undershot bites vary in degree. Severe distortion shows up early in life, whereas less severe degrees emerge later. In one Beagle line, a mild undershot position can be a transient phase between four and six months of age, correcting with the achievement of full growth. In one known instance, a minimally undershot bite appeared at about one year of age and became permanent.

It is an unfortunate truth that some ever-inventive exhibitors resort to various devices to achieve the appearance of a good bite. Surgical realignment of the front teeth, grinding of the upper or lower incisors, use of orthodontic appliances and rubber bands have apparently all been used. Apart from the fact that it is violation of AKC rules to physically alter the appearance of a dog, bad bites are most likely an inherited trait. A dog with an "enhanced" bite will still carry the blemish in its genes, ready to pass them to the next generation. So what has really been accomplished?

WHICH DO I KEEP?

Usually, there is one pup or, if you are lucky two, in a litter that catches your eye right from birth. Often, these same puppies at twelve weeks will continue to stand out.

If you are exceptionally lucky, all your pups may appear to be good show prospects. What you keep for future breeding depends on what improvements you want to make in your line.

In our tightly bred line, for example, the Beagles tended toward a short, heavy neck and higher ear set, and the thirteen-inch bitches had some trouble whelping. Therefore, when the choice was made in a later litter, a fifteen-inch, leggy, long-eared bitch with good reach of neck was retained, while two smaller but actually better overall bitches went to new homes.

Nothing can match the fun of showing your homebred Beagle to its championship and beyond. It is every breeder's dream to breed an outstanding Beagle that makes its mark in the ring and on its progeny. With luck, you may get both in one package.

Good bitches are the mainstay of any breeding program. If space limitations prevent you from keeping a good bitch from each carefully planned breeding, then the bitch can be placed with breeding rights. This system has worked well for many breeders, who then whelp and raise litters before returning bitches to their homes. Our practice was to keep both a bitch and a dog from a particularly good litter. Unless you plan to keep one of the off-spring of a particular mating, or unless you have specific requests for pups from that breeding, do not breed. The world is full of wonderful Beagles—so many that some end up in Beagle rescue programs.

"I Want a Best in Show Puppy . . . "

. . . is the naive demand of many a prospective puppy buyer—but don't we all! Let's face it: The only way you can be assured of a Best in Show Beagle is to buy one—the Beagle, that is.

Group and Best in Show wins depend on a number of factors, not the least of which are luck and timing. All a responsible breeder can guarantee a prospective buyer of a promising puppy is good health and good tempera-ment when the purchase involves a twelve- or thirteen-week-old puppy. However, if the puppy is the product of a repeat breeding where the previous litter has reached adulthood, more accurate predictions of adult conforma-tion and show-worthiness can be made.

BUYER'S AND SELLER'S RIGHTS

A written contract spelling out all the conditions of sale is essential. The new owner must be assured of a healthy, sociable Beagle with a life-long commitment from the breeder to accept the Beagle back if circumstances re-quire. The breeder, in turn, needs a spay/neuter contract if the Beagle is not to be bred and assurance of a good home for the puppy with the proviso that the Beagle be returned if the situation warrants. Divorce, illness and death do unfortunately happen in families, making placement of the family Beagle necessary.

Two types of registration of the puppy are offered by the American Ken-nel Club: *full* and *limited*. The latter prohibits registration of any offspring if the Beagle, at some time in the future, is bred in contravention of the spay/neuter agreement.

A "dowry" consisting of the following should accompany the puppy to its new home: health history, record of vaccinations and worming, AKC reg-istration papers (unless a spay/neuter contract required documentation from the operating veterinarian), pedigree, feeding instructions, vaccination sched-ule, grooming instructions and the names of good local veterinarians and puppy trainers. A supply of food for the first few days, some favorite toys and a blanket or towel to supply the familiar odor of home will help ease the adjustment of the puppy to its new home.

R.D.'s Perpetual Motion, thirteen-inch dog (Ch. R.D.'s Strike It Rich ex Ch. Cedar Breaks My Magic Muffin), owned by Ardie Haydon and Karen Crary. *Callea*

Brushy Run Lil' Buccaneer (Ch. Pin Oaks Lil' Buckaroo ex Brushy Run Lanny's Choice), at ten weeks, is an excellent example of combined show and field breeding. *Kristine Kraeuter*

Ch. Kahootz Chase Manhattan, thirteen-inch dog (Ch. Shaw's Spirit of the Chase ex Ch. Just-Wright Run to You), a multiple Group and Specialty Variety winner, owned by C. Diaz M. Austin, A. Williams and J. Wood. *Callea*

chapter 11

Puppy Training for Home and Show Ring

SOCIALIZATION

Once puppies begin to see and hear at about three weeks of age, they embark on the most critical period of their lives for their social development. From three weeks to ten weeks, the pups learn about people, noises, and new environmental experiences, with the peak of socialization occurring between five weeks and seven weeks.

Regular playtime with the pups and a gradual extension of their world from whelping box to pen to small room, with occasional visits to other parts of the house and outdoors as weather permits, provide pups with optimal exposure. Supervised visits from friends, neighbors and children introduce new human smells and contacts. Toothproof toys—chew sticks, knotted socks (NO nylon stockings or pantyhose) and sturdy stuffed toys—entertain both Beagles and owners and encourage chewing on designated objects, not fingers. A radio or TV tuned to talk shows in the puppy room adds another important exposure.

The Campbell Puppy Behavior Test (q.v.) gives an objective evaluation of each pup's personality at six weeks of age. Five simple tasks, performed in a test area, will confirm your initial impression of the degrees of dominance/submission patterns in each puppy. The five tasks follow:

1. Attracting the pup by clapping hands
2. Walking away from the pup to check its desire to follow
3. Holding the pup down on its back gently for thirty seconds to observe struggling or docility

4. Petting the puppy from top of head downward along the neck and back

5. Cradling the pup in the palm of the hands with the fingers interlaced and elevating it

Responses are graded as shown.

This information makes deciding what kind of family to place a particular puppy with much easier. The rankings for the Campbell Test follow:

dd	Dominant dominance
s	Submissive
d	Dominant
ss	Strongly submissive
i	Inhibited

The dominant dominance pup (two or more *dd* responses and *d* in the remainder) will react in a dominant, aggressive way and, with proper training, will fit best with a calm, adult family.

The dominant pup (three or more *d* responses) will be an outgoing, quick learner.

Those with three or more *s* responses are more submissive and work well with small children and older folks.

The highly submissive pup (three or more *ss* responses, especially with an *i*) needs consistent and gentle handling to adjust nicely with a family.

Those pups with two or more *i* responses, when associated with some *dd* and *d* responses, may attack if stressed by traditional punishment; whereas those associated with some *i*, accompanied by some *ss* or *s* responses, will tend to be shy under pressure.

We have yet to see a Beagle puppy that falls into the latter category. The vast majority of Beagles fall somewhere between moderately dominant and mildly submissive. Those highly or moderately dominant make the best show prospects. Those with tail-down responses can be brought along in the show ring with careful, gentle handling.

Remember that the best training system is one that rewards acceptable behavior and ignores that which is unacceptable.

PUPPY BEHAVIOR TEST (CAMPBELL)
Score Sheet

SECTION NUMBER AND PUP BEHAVIOR

1. **Social Attraction**

Came readily—tail up—jumped—bit at hands	*dd*
Came readily—tail up—pawed at hands	*d*
Came readily—tail down	*s*
Came, hesitant—tail down	*ss*
Did not come at all	*i*

2. **Following**

Followed readily—tail up—underfoot—bit at feet	*dd*
Followed readily—tail up—underfoot	*d*
Followed readily—tail down	*s*
Followed, hesitant—tail down	*ss*
Did not follow or went away	*i*

3. **Restraint Dominance (30 seconds)**

Struggled fiercely—flailed—bit	*dd*
Struggled fiercely—flailed	*d*
Struggled, then settled	*s*
No struggle—licked hands	*ss*

4. **Social Dominance (30 seconds)**

Jumped—pawed—bit—growled	*dd*
Jumped—pawed	*d*
Squirmed—licked at hands	*s*
Rolled over—licked at hands	*ss*
Went away and stayed away	*i*

5. **Elevation Dominance (30 seconds)**

Struggled fiercely—bit—growled	*dd*
Struggled fiercely	*d*
Struggled—settled—licked	*s*
No struggle—licked at hands	*ss*

PUPPY TRAINING

Getting off on the right foot with a new puppy requires some clear idea on proper training methods.

Beagle puppies want to please their human friends, and it is best to use this as the basis of a training strategy. Dogs learn best by being rewarded for appropriate behavior with praise and food treats; punishment is cruel and abusive. Dogs can learn easily what certain words mean. For example, "outside" is the signal for where to go for urination and defecation; "no," on the other hand, gives the puppy no clear signal as to what *is* expected.

There are an enormous number of tasks a new puppy must learn: where to relieve itself, what areas of the house are off limits, when and when not to bark, which items may be chewed on, how to walk on a leash and a number of specific commands. "Come," "sit," "stay," "outside," "down" and "stand" can all be life-saving.

No wonder there are occasional mistakes.

Teaching your puppy early to feel at home with the handling of its mouth, head, ears and feet makes grooming chores and veterinary visits much easier for all concerned. Many communities offer puppy-training classes, giving puppy and owner a chance to learn these important canine life skills.

CONFORMATION TRAINING

In the show ring, the Beagle must stand for the judge's examination, trot on a lead with head and tail up and "free-stack" or stand in show stance on its own with tail and head up. The same training principles apply here that work for general training. Reward your Beagle's proper behavior with praise and rewards. Ignore his undesirable behavior.

Stacking experience and training can begin as early as four weeks of age. Simply postition your pup in the proper stance for several seconds randomly throughout the day on an elevated surface—bed, countertop, washing machine—anything will do. Praise the puppy lavishly when it stands still for even a moment. Gradually, the pup will stand for longer periods. Always make each stacking session brief, and be sure to quit while you are ahead!

When your Beagle can stand for half a minute or so, other household members can play "judge," handling its head, examining the bite, feeling for shoulder layback and (if appropriate) the presence of testicles.

Collar training begins at three weeks of age with the use of a small, soft puppy collar. By the time the litter has learned to chew the collars off, the lesson has been painlessly learned.

Six weeks of age is the best time to start lead training. Let the pups run around a bit with a soft leather show lead on each, ends dragging on the floor or ground. The baby Beagles love it.

When they appear comfortable with the leads, enlist the aid of family members or friends as auxiliary handlers. Tug gently on the lead, coaxing each puppy along, praising it as it follows. Don't worry if its nose is to the ground. After all, that's natural Beagles behavior, and it is a scent hound. Small bits of puppy chow work well as treats for tasks well done. Having the puppies follow their dam on a lead works well, too.

Brief, daily training periods initially fix the pattern so the puppy knows what is expected when show training begins in earnest. These practice sessions should be fun for you and the puppy. Recruit neighbors and local children to accustom the pups to being handled by strangers.

As the puppy progresses, follow the standard conformation-ring routine: stack, gait around a large circle, as well as down and back; "make a triangle" and stop in a show pose. This latter step is impressive when seen in the ring.

Initially offer treats while each task is being mastered. Later, with your Beagle in the ring, Dr. Ian Dunbar suggests that treats be offered intermittently for successful performance. This keeps the dog guessing and eager, not sure just when its treat will magically appear. Unbroken repetition becomes boring for your dog, too.

Since the Beagle Standard includes a height disqualification, familiarize your Beagle with measuring procedures as well. In this way, it will respond properly if the judge decides to call a measure on your hound.

Puppy matches accustom a young Beagle to travel and the sights and sounds of the dog-show scene. Enjoy these excursions with your budding show star, but make sure they are not too exhausting. Remember, your Beagle is still just a baby.

Owners busy with jobs, family responsibilities and several dogs don't always have time for a daily practice session. If the puppy has had a good basic training experience, brief refresher courses prior to the start of its show career work well.

Unfortunately, experiences that can be startling or frightening to a dog can easily occur at dog shows. Heavy paraphernalia can fall with attendant, horrendous clatter. Onlookers scream, shout and applaud suddenly and loudly. Two dogs suddenly begin fighting loudly right behind you and your dog in the ring. Give the puppy a chance to collect itself. Beagles are pretty resilient, but some are of softer temperament than others. Know your own hound and help it react to these non-emergencies with style.

On the other hand, rewarding spooky behavior—tail down, cringing or flattening on the ground—by fussing or coddling teaches the young dog the wrong lesson. Ignore the "nervous Nellie" act and go about your business of signaling that the unexpected furor is no reason to come unglued.

Aus. Ch. Filnor Songbird, fifteen-inch bitch (Aus. Ch. Nangunyah Smokescreen ex Aus. Ch. Filnor Prima Donna), one of Austrailia's top-winning bitches, owned by Mrs. Norma Shipley. *R. May*

chapter 12

Good Care of Your Beagle

Good preventive veterinary care includes a current vaccination program, annual checkups, and visits as needed for problems as they arise.

At home, some simple healthcare tasks should be performed on a regular basis.

GROOMING

Ear cleaning, toenail trimming, brushing or stripping out dead coat, cleaning teeth and expressing anal glands should be done monthly or more often if needed. Baths are given as often as necessary.

Ears—Because of the Beagle's pendulous ears, ear-mite infestation is common. Cleaning the inside of the ears—the ear canal—gently with cotton swabs and alcohol removes dust, superficial wax and debris. One-half eyedropperful of a 1:3 mixture of Canex™ or Canolene™ to mineral oil in each ear, followed by gentle massage, once monthly seems to prevent the development of ear-mite infestation. An offensive odor or discharge from the ear requires a trip to the veterinarian. Ear infections can be difficult to clear.

Nails—An active Beagle running on hard surfaces wears its nails down naturally. The more sedentary elderly Beagle, of course, will require more frequent attention to its nails. Short nails result in a tight, compact foot; long nails can get caught and torn, and this can be extremely painful. Nails can be kept short by cutting with a nail clipper or grinding with an electric grinder. Never cut or grind beyond the tip of the pink nail bed or "quick," which is visible within the nail. This can result in copious bleeding and a hound that learns to be troublesome about foot care. It is wiser to take off

145

only a very small amount each time. Eventually, the quicks will recede, giving the look you want to the foot.

Anal glands—Anal-gland expression is not the most pleasant of tasks. These glands, located on either side of the anus, secrete a foul-smelling substance. If they get plugged or impacted, infection can set in, resulting in a painful abscess. Using several thicknesses of facial tissue, you can squeeze firmly on both sides of the anus to express the secretions.

Bathing—Bathing need not be an ordeal. Beagles, like people, prefer their water warm and don't like soap in their eyes, ears or mouth. Flea and tick shampoos contain various insecticides, so follow your veterinarian's recommendations as to which product can be used safely with your particular flea-prevention program. A good sudsing, followed by a thorough rinsing, brisk toweling and complete drying in a warm, dry room leaves your Beagle "squeaky clean."

CARE OF THE TEETH

Care of your Beagle's teeth requires brushing with a soft toothbrush and a veterinary toothpaste or gel at least twice a week, preferably daily. Use of a salt-and-soda paste also works to slow tartar accumulation but may not be as tasty to the dog. Tooth scalers for heavier tartar removal are helpful, but some skill is needed to master the technique of their use.

Reward your Beagle with a treat after these brushing procedures; he will love it. Ours even line up eagerly to have their teeth brushed and squabble over which will be first!

In spite of your best efforts, sooner or later cleaning under anesthesia by your veterinarian will be necessary. Pockets of infection under the gum line can lead to the spread of infection to other parts of the body, primarily the lungs and kidneys.

EXERCISE

Beagle puppies and young adults romp and play with great enthusiasm. A good run or play session in the morning, afternoon and before bedtime keeps your dog happy and well-exercised.

As the Beagle grows older, a good walk twice a day ensures better health for you both. Beagles with chronic disc disease or chronic heart problems will tolerate much less exercise. Follow your veterinarian's advice with these old-timers.

FLEA CONTROL

No doubt the most discouraging problem you will have to deal with is the tiny flea. A scourge to man and beast, the flea is a real survivor. It will drive you and your Beagle crazy.

Regular spraying of your yard and flea-bombing your home during the "flea season" will help keep the population down. Both oral and topical products administered once monthly are now available for your Beagle. One targets the flea eggs, the other the adults. Your veterinarian can keep you up-to-date with current recommendations. These new products may eliminate the need for insecticide dips and sprays.

WEIGHT CONTROL

If given the opportunity, any healthy, usually ravenous Beagle will literally eat itself to death.

Obesity complicates any existing illness, predisposes your dog to disc and joint problems and is absolutely within your control. It is much easier to keep your Beagle at a proper weight than it is to try dieting down from a five- to ten-pound excess. That can take months. A subcutaneous fat layer of about one-half inch over the rib cage is as much as your Beagle needs. When in doubt, weigh.

IDENTIFICATION

Permanent identification of your Beagle is essential. Stray Beagles can be readily identified and returned to their owners. Ownership can be proven if questioned.

Several methods are available. Tattooing a number either on the tummy or inside the ear has been a common technique. Various registries provide a databank of these numbers, but knowing which registry to consult can sometimes be a problem.

More recently, implantation of a coded microchip between a dog's shoulder blades has proven very effective, though several registries are available for this method as with tattooing. The American Kennel Club's databank is a simple, inexpensive tool. Most rescue agencies have scanners available that can provide the number to be matched with the registry's.

At this writing, it is probable that the American Kennel Club will eventually require proof of identification before individual registration is accepted. This will be via the microchip.

Ch. Starbuck's Hang 'Em High, fifteen-inch dog (Ch. The Whim's Buckeye ex Ch. Elsy's Shooting Star), owned by David and Linda Hiltz, has carved himself a permanent place in the history of the breed. The top Beagle sire of all time with 123 champions, he was also a top winner with twenty-three Bests in Show and eleven Specialty Bests of Breed. He was NBC Sire of the Year for 1980-1984, and Beagle of the Year, 1980. *Missy Yuhl*

THE GERIATRIC BEAGLE

Beagles live longer than many of the large dog breeds. The average life span is about fourteen years, with some hardy souls making it to seventeen years. Beagle owners are lucky in that respect.

Most Beagles begin to slow down at around age twelve years. Annual check-ups, increased to twice yearly at about ten years, bring to light any developing physical problems. Proper diet and continuing regular exercise geared to the older Beagle's tolerance, as well as avoidance of unnecessary stresses, can add quality time to his life.

Failing hearing and sight are inevitable. Old Beagles that by accident wander from home may not hear or see oncoming cars. Extra attention therefore is required when workpeople or servicepeople are about your home, leaving doors or gates open. This one of those times that a crate is so helpful and a crate-trained dog is such a plus.

Ch. Saga's Critic's Choice, fifteen-inch bitch, and Ch. Saga's Top Cat, fifteen-inch dog. Owned by Ada T. Lueke.

Changes in routine are more upsetting to old-timers, and they may become cranky with younger dogs. They tend to sleep a great deal, require fewer calories, and arthritic stiffness and muscle wasting prevent comfortable exercise. Many old Beagles show signs of intervertebral disc disease (degeneration and/or extrusion of the cushion between the vertebral bodies).

A group of Danish and Swedish Beagles enjoying the coast at Bornholm, Sweden. *Karen Ulrich*

The onset of graying around the eyes and muzzle depends on the individual family. Some show grizzling as early as two or three years, whereas others don't show until eight or nine.

Small skin tumors become evident at about ten years, growing in all sorts of places and in all sizes and shapes. Most lumps are perfectly benign, but, unfortunately, not all. Fast-developing growths should be removed. Black tumors, especially on the mucous membranes of the mouth, should always be removed and histological sections done. Malignant melanoma, a rapidly growing and spreading tumor, is a not-uncommon cause of death in older Beagles.

With decreasing blood supply to the brain, the old Beagle may show signs of senility similar to those seen in humans. Incontinence, loss of house-training habits and nocturnal restlessness often with episodes of persistent barking can try the patience of the most devoted of owners. Jacob Mosier, DVM, reports that sometimes a twenty-four-hour course of oxygen therapy can provide a temporary return (up to several months) to more normal functioning.

Early treatment of any developing physical problem, such as heart, kidney or liver disease, can add years to your Beagle's life. For the deteriorating heart valve, identified by development of a murmur, a change to a low-salt diet and medications to reduce the work load on the heart can delay the onset of heart failure.

Proper dietary protein regulation will aid ailing kidneys, and thyroid supplement will be required for hypothyroidism, a common occurrence in middle-aged Beagles.

In those Beagles with epilepsy that have averaged one to three seizures per year, the frequency of seizures may *decrease* significantly with the use of appropriate medication properly administered.

Two kinds of transient neurological episodes have occurred in some of our old-timers. The first is the sudden onset of a drooping lower eyelid in combination with a constricted pupil. This condition, known as Horner's syndrome, usually clears completely within several weeks without any treatment. The second looks like a small stroke and probably is. The Beagle may appear unsteady and confused and have difficulty getting up. Initially, you may think you are seeing an epileptic seizure, but the symptoms persist for several hours. Usually, all symptoms clear by eight to ten hours, and your Beagle is himself again. Your veterinarian should be notified, however, when one of these episodes occurs.

Hospitalization is particularly difficult for the elderly Beagle. Frequent visits by the owner, a familiar blanket and early "discharge" to home nursing can help.

When old organs fail or malignancy is winning the battle, the decision to euthanize your old friend must be made. It is so difficult to know exactly when. Sadly, most of us wait too long. Pain, failure of appetite and "no joy in life" mark the time.

Euthanasia in the Beagle's home is best, but not always possible. I (JM) need to hold my old-timers when my veterinarian gives the last injection. They deserve that much.

Remember that this is also a difficult task for your veterinarian, who has cared for your Beagle over many years. Sometimes an associate in the same office is a kinder choice.

A 1995 health survey of the National Beagle Club of America Supporting Membership indicated that cancer and multiple organ failure (old age) are the primary causes of death in the breed.

Ch. Starbuck's Meadow Song, fifteen-inch bitch (Ch. The Whim's Buckeye ex Ch. Elsy's Shooting Star), an outstanding producer of many Best in Show champions, reprised her career at age sixteen in the Parade of Champions at the 1993 NBC Specialty. This grand veteran is shown with her proud owner, Annette Didier. *Kim Booth*

chapter 13

Grooming for the Show Ring—An Illustrated Guide

Though the Beagle is a short-coated dog, trimming can enhance the outline and present a cleaner line to the animal. Personally, we prefer the more natural look that a scissors trim can give to the "clippered" look. So the following is offered as instructions to achieve the former approach.

EQUIPMENT NEEDED

Grooming table or two stacked crates with a nonskid surface and grooming arm

Good source of light, either daylight or artificial

Comb (combination fine and coarse teeth)

Straight-edged barber scissors

Thinning shears (44-20 brand Taper Fine)

Nail clippers or electric grinder

Terrier stripping knife (fine teeth)

Small, curved, blunt-ended scissors

Hound glove

You will also need certain items for emergencies: eye ointment or drops, coagulant (to stop bleeding), oral antibiotics, antidiarrhea medication and cortisone cream (for "hot spots" or foot irritations).

To make pill-giving easy (at shows or at home), put the pill in a small ball of cold cream cheese and offer it to your Beagle as a treat.

Dan. Ch. Susquatch Rhythm 'N Blues, fifteen-inch dog
(Dutch/KLB Ch. Fiery Flash Little Big Man ex Susquatch
Cashew Special), one of Denmark's top-winning Beagles,
owned by Karen and Marianne Ulrich.

THE GROOMING PROCESS

Depending on the thickness and length of your Beagle's coat, trimming should begin at least four weeks before show time, and sometimes as early as three months if the coat is particularly thick and heavy ("winter coat" syndrome). The finishing touches, such as fine tuning ears, pasterns and feet, of course, can wait until the day before the show. The major tasks with respect to the coat should begin early, because you will need to repeat them weekly. If your Beagle grows a heavy undercoat, the stripping process may need to be performed every other day or even daily to remove the unwanted portion.

Head

Eyes: Remove the "fuzz" at the inner corner of the eyes with thinning shears.

Ears: Smooth the edge of the ears with scissors and blend the trimmed area with the rest of the ear, as shown in Figure 1A.

Whiskers: Although we no longer trim whiskers, since they are tactile organs that the dog should have, they can be removed, if desired, with scissors.

Lips: Smooth the edge of the upper lip with scissors.

Neck

Start trimming the neck on either side with a good, sharp pair of thinning shears, beginning just below the ear, about on line with the back edge of attachment to the skull. Gradually cut the hair away from the surface. Do *not* stick the thinning shears upward under the coat and cut hunks of hair out, because in time, this will produce an irregular, lumpy, chopped look (see Figures 1B and 2).

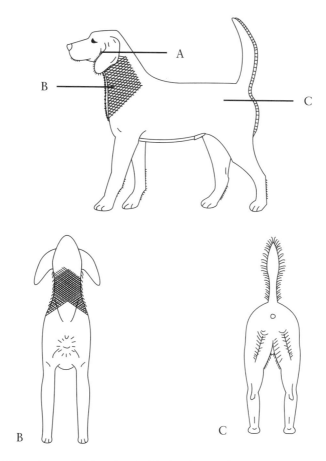

Grooming and Trimming Guide for the Beagle in the Show Ring

Gradually trim the coat downward toward the shoulder and, if necessary, over the shoulder and down onto the chest. Your goal is to clean up the lines of the neck and chest.

Many dogs have a "ruff" partway down the neck onto the shoulder, and this should be trimmed neatly and blended in.

Repeat the entire process on the opposite side.

A very important component in properly grooming a Beagle is stripping out the undercoat, as well as all the dead hair. Removal of this unsightly hair will enhance the glossiness of the coat. After the neck has been trimmed, it will appear as though all the color in a dark-coated dog has been removed. However, if you are diligent and keep up the trimming on a regular basis, along with judicious stripping out of the undercoat, you will be surprised how the color will return. Obviously, this work cannot be done a day or so before the show, but should be done well in advance, with maintenance kept up throughout the interval.

Ch. Whiskey Creek's Headliner, fifteen-inch dog (Ch. White Acres I'm Heavenly Too ex Ch. Whiskey Creek's N Erin's Maddy Hays), multiple Best in Show and Specialty winner, owned by M. Delia and M. Sager. *JC Photo*

Am. & Aus. Ch. Tashwould First Warning, fifteen-inch bitch (Ch. Torbay Final Fling ex Am. & Can. Ch. Merry Song's High Spirit), owned by David and Lesley Hiltz, is a multiple Group winner and Runner-up BIS winner in Australia. She continued her winning ways after arriving in the United States, adding Group placements and Specialty wins. *Booth*

Blend your trimming of the neck into the chest smoothly. Crosshatched areas on the drawings in this chapter show the areas to be trimmed.

Chest

Using scissors, smooth the center line over the front of the chest.

Abdomen

Trim closely with scissors to develop a smooth arch line in front of the thigh. For a male, carefully trim long hairs from the sheath and pelvic area.

Hindquarters

Develop a nice outward arch to the buttocks from the base of the tail downward toward the stifle. Using thinning shears, gradually trim the coat in this area to get a clean line from both side and rear. The buttocks should show a smooth, convex line. Get all the excess hair off, as illustrated in Figures 1 and 3.

Next, develop a concave or inward curve over the stifle area. Color, both over buttocks and stifles, can be of help in determining how much to trim. You don't want to trim the buttocks, for example, so much that they appear narrow when viewed from the side.

Also trim the fuzzy hair from the inside of the thighs for a clean, trim look (see Figure 3).

Tail

With a combination of thinning shears and scissors, start an upward line from just above the anus (see Figures 1C and 3C), and carry it up in a smooth curve to about one-third the length of the tail. Make this line a smooth transition into the brush. *Do not square off the tail tip;* leave it pointed smoothly, as in the natural state. The tail should be smooth, not irregular.

Feet

Trim around the outside of the feet and between the pads. Nails should be clipped or ground back gradually.

Pasterns

Trimming with scissors should be done so that, when observed from the side, the pastern is straight up and down from the fetlock to the pad. Some of the irregular hair along the back of the front leg can also be trimmed.

Teeth

Teeth should be clean. This can be achieved by regular brushing at home using a canine dentifrice or paste of salt and bicarbonate of soda along with a soft toothbrush. If necessary, more recalcitrant tartar can be scraped or chipped away with a dental scaler.

Ears

Regular attention to ears to prevent ear-mite infestation or accumulation of the waxy cerumen will ensure clean, healthy ears. A cleanup prior to being shown will generally prevent the dog from shaking his head when the show lead is in place.

Removal of Urine Stains

With some Beagles, there may be a problem with urine stains on feet and tail. To remove them, make a paste of equal parts of vinegar and water mixed with cornstarch. Rub it into the stained areas and leave it on overnight. Brush out thoroughly in the morning.

CONDITIONING

Obviously, proper conditioning for superior ring readiness is the result of good diet, sensible weight control, plenty of exercise and general attention to the dog's health. Uncomfortable travel arrangements will also take their toll, so be sure that the dog is comfortable on its way to a show, especially if it must be shipped by air. The airline crate should be properly roomy and should have a water supply either during hot weather or for long distances. Fill a rabbit/guinea pig water bottle and attach it to the crate door so that the water will drip into the plastic dish that is also usually attached to the door. Movement of the crate will allow the water supply to drip gradually, or the dog can lick the tip of the water bottle.

Frozen cold packs wrapped in freezer bags beneath the crate's floor covering will also help keep a dog cool and comfortable in warm weather.

Beagle Rescue

The purebred dog population has exploded during the last thirty-five years. An unfortunate consequence of this phenomenon is the growing number of purebreds being abandoned or surrendered to humane societies. In an attempt to save these victims of our "disposable society" from extermination, many breed clubs have developed "rescue initiatives" for their specific breeds. Attempts are made to locate the owner of the dog if the animal is a stray. If the dog has been turned in to the local pound or The Humane Society, a call is made to the breed-rescue contact. If possible, the dog is taken by club rescue and placement and a new home is located after neutering or spaying the rescued animal.

Beagle rescue became organized in 1977. Southern California Beagle Club developed a rescue program about the same time that Mary Powell and Trudi Reveira (Powveira Beagles) launched a service in Northern California. Since then, two Beagle Clubs, Rocky Mountain and Columbia-Willamette, plus Linda Forrest (The Tavern's Beagles) with her SOS Beagle Rescue serving the central East Coast have joined the effort. In 1995, through the encouragement of Ted Swedalla and Terri Giannetti (Beowulf Beagles), the National Beagle Club held its first annual fund-raising event for rescue support. Two auctions have been held since in conjunction with the National Specialty Show and have proven very successful.

From time to time, individuals have contributed several years of rescue independent of any breed organization.

These efforts have been costly, exhausting and both heart-breaking and rewarding. Though initially a club function, Southern California Beagle Club's rescue evolved into its current status: an operation independent of the Club, handled by Janet and Bill Nieland (Nieland's Beagles). A similar transformation occurred after four years with Rocky Mountain Beagle Club's rescue.

Ch. Red Baron's Gorgeous Sunny Girl, fifteen-inch bitch (Dan. & JGD Ch. Sweet Connection's Bar Expresso ex Dan. Ch. Magic Noire Sunshine Baroness). Group winner and NBC Specialty Award of Merit winner, 1996, owned by Annette Didier.

Aus. Ch. Toonhound Spring Colours, fifteen-inch dog (Am. Ch. Starbuck Torbay Colours ex Aus. Ch. Toonhound Spring Bonnet), owned by Mr. D. Coffey, is a Group and BIS winner and was BOB at the prestigious Sydney Royal show in 1996. *Cobal*

Ch. Brushy Run Cornchips, thirteen-inch dog (Ch. Wishing Well's Burnt Popcorn ex Del-View Pinie) hunts with the Holly Hill Pack Beagles and is owned by Wanda Borsa and Kris Kraeuter. *Ashbey*

Incorporating in 1995 as Colorado Beagle Rescue, an independent not-for-profit organization, the club's current officers are Sylvia Rushforth, President; Carol Larmore, Treasurer and Ardie Haydon, Consultant. A computerized tracking system has been developed for Beagles placed.

So far, Columbia-Willamette Beagle Club's rescue service lies within the club. Jean Applegate and now Bridget Roth have headed an informal limited program attempting to match the relinquishing owner with a prospective owner by phone.

SOS Beagle Rescue is also an independent, not-for-profit organization. As with all rescue programs, funds for spaying and neutering, veterinary fees and temporary boarding or foster-family placement come from donations from the adopting families. Sometimes a fee is required from the relinquishing owner as well.

Blossom Valley Beagle Club contributes to the Northern California Beagle Rescue with proceeds from an annual raffle.

In addition, almost all the Beaglers running the rescue services are involved in efforts to track down local puppy mills, educate the public and pressure Beagle breeders to assume responsibility for *all* the Beagles they produce, including those sired by their studs.

HOW MANY?

The statistics regarding numbers alone are horrifying. For example, Northern California Beagle Rescue placed **130** Beagles in 1996 with an approximate total of **1,500** since 1977. When the experimental Beagle colony at the University of California-Davis was disbanded, 60 Beagles ranging in age from six months to fifteen years were funneled into regional animal shelters for placement. A concerted effort on the part of local Humane Societies and Powell and Reveira resulted in all being placed. Remember—these Beagles had never been socialized, were wary of humans and had never even been out of their colony except for research procedures. What a tribute to the Beagle spirit that these dogs ultimately adapted to family life.

Colorado Beagle Rescue and Rocky Mountain Beagle Club placed **170** Beagles since 1991.

Janet Nieland (Southern California Beagle Rescue) reports ten to fifteen calls per week from owners wanting to place their Beagles. In 1996, thirty-seven hounds were placed successfully. One, Chester, did not adapt during three tries with different owners but proved a great success with the Beagle Brigade, the Department of Agriculture's contraband food-sniffer program. Chester and his handler are stationed at post offices during the day.

WHERE DO THESE BEAGLES COME FROM?

More than 50 percent of the rescued Beagles come from animal shelters, about another 40 percent are turned in by their owners and 10 percent are held by owners until placement is made. The majority are products of pet store sales and backyard breeders. Unfortunately, in some areas, the percentage of Beagles produced by breeders who do not take responsibility for taking their sold stock back is rising.

A frightening new development is the use of the Internet to advertise puppies and stud service.

Buyer beware!

chapter 15

Genetics: How Can I Use What I Don't Understand?

Well, the happy news is that you don't have to be a geneticist to apply genetic principles. The purpose of this chapter is to give the breeder a way to work with the laws of heredity in a practical fashion.

Remember as you read this chapter that the key to the system hinges on consistency and focus. In other words, determine what you want and adhere to it, and don't try to solve all your problems at once.

BREEDING CO-OPS

Since most dog fanciers are limited in physical breeding facilities, we recommend the idea of a co-op breeding program. The idea is to link up with two or three others who agree with your ideas of what the perfect dog should be, establish a list of priorities and work on them together. One or two good studs and several bitches can not only increase your chances for success but also accelerate your time frame considerably.

All the Beagles you are breeding from should have the same general conformation or "type" and should be appealing to all the breeders involved. If you could cut and paste, you must be able to make the perfect dog with these starter animals. That is, no one fault should appear in all the dogs. After the first or second round of breeding, you should be able to determine which of your bitches are going to be the best producers.

CULLING ETHICS AND BREEDER RESPONSIBILITY

The greatest problem for the breeder is not selecting the good puppies but culling out the puppies that exhibit undesirable traits. It seems to be our cross to bear that we breed a gorgeous puppy with at least one ghastly fault or inherited defect, or a not-so-great puppy with a spectacular virtue. This is the hardest part of breeding, because our hearts are so in control of our heads.

If all we are going to do is neuter these puppies, keep them and love them, fine. But if we loose control of our plan, the improvement of the breed is never going to become a reality.

Most breeds have some hereditary problems that their breeders would rather not deal with at all, and Beagles are no exception. But conscientious breeders meet the challenge of hereditary defects head on. They look for straight answers from their veterinarians and consultants on the nature of these defects in their breeding programs. A failure to face hereditary problems as they arise can only lead to more trouble in the future. We are all tempted to overlook a fault in a "superpup," particularly if he only carries it in recessive, so it is not visible. However, to linebreed and especially to inbreed, one must be heartless and cull dedicatedly.

In the canine world as a whole, and the Beagle world in particular, there is a general unwillingness to admit that genetic problems exist. There can be no upgrading with a specific problem if Beagle owners and breeders refuse to admit that there really are problems to be faced. It is all well and good to talk about the promotion and improvement of Beagles, but we can do this only if owners are scrupulously honest in their dealings with one another.

Some of the factors that will retard progress in reducing the incidence of genetic problems follow:

- Ignoring a problem
- Rationalizing the inheritability of a problem
- Basing a breeding program on insufficient/incorrect data
- Dishonesty about the carrier status of one's dog
- Breaking down honest communication by gossiping and witch-hunting

With early detection of affected individuals and their removal from the breeding population, you can reduce the chance of increasing the problems those hounds bring to the gene pool. If you avoid breeding from affected dogs, your action must inevitably result in fewer carriers being born and in a lower number of affected puppies being produced.

Even when the exact mode of inheritance for a particular trait is a puzzle to the breeder, the principle of heredity can be followed with a well-thought-out plan and specific goals to accomplish.

A BREEDING SYSTEM

Given that only a small number of gene pairs that produce the qualities breeders are interested in have been identified and their mode of inheritance worked out, and given the number of puppies it would take to get the qualities breeders desire, there are no easy answers. How—or maybe the question should be why—then should breeders use the genetic knowledge available to them?

First, keep in mind that all dogs are more or less inbred; you could get St. Bernards instead of Beagles when your bitch has a litter. This makes the job a little easier.

Second, as a breeder, you have three very powerful tools at your disposal: inbreeding, outcrossing and selection. Linebreeding is a form of inbreeding. With a well-thought-out program, these three devices can improve the quality of your stock rather rapidly.

Here's the system:

1. Make a list of traits and decide which are essential and which are intolerable. Rank these traits in order of importance.
2. Be clear in your mind what it is you are looking for in a particular breeding and stick with it until you get it. In other words, set clear goals.
3. Develop a scoring system that can easily be carried out.
4. Linebreed or inbreed to the best animal produced until a better one in respect to the qualities that you have given top priority comes along. Then breed to that one.

That's the whole thing in a nutshell—everything else are ruffles and flourishes on that theme.

The steps to getting what you want are easy. It's the implementation that gets tough because of the sheer volume of records and the strict need for objectivity.

You should plan a breeding program in a positive manner, breeding for desired traits. However, faults can spoil an otherwise promising breeding animal, so you must give them attention as well.

We suggest that you start with dogs of overall correct English Foxhound type. Then decide what single or at most what two faults you want to eliminate or improve on and work to that end while maintaining the overall correct appearance. After all, you do have to live with these dogs on a daily basis, and they might as well be pleasing to the eye while they are there for you to see!

The genotype or genetic constitution of an organism including genes without visible manifestation is determined partially by what is seen and by what the animal produces, as well as by the growing number of diseases that can be tested for in the laboratory.

Try to keep your goals simple. Your chances for success will be greater if you don't try to breed for or against too many qualities all at once. The ideal would be to select for one thing at a time. This is what agricultural breeders do, and so should you. Unfortunately, you are not looking for just one

Ch. Saga's Donnybrook, fifteen-inch dog (Ch. Page Mill On The Road Again ex Ch. Saga's Critic's Choice), owned by Ada T. Lueke, has Hound Group placements but doesn't like getting too far from his own "personal Beagle."

quality, such as egg production or quantity of meat on the hoof, but the idea is the same. If you get and keep these one or two traits in successive generations, consider yourself very fortunate.

For selection purposes, a minimum acceptable level must be established, and all dogs kept as breeding stock must be above the minimum accepted standard you have established for all traits being considered. However, there must be some flexibility to ensure that you have enough replacement dogs to maintain a stable population size.

Selection is probably the most important single tool you will use. You must cull your puppies based on objectivity, not sentimentality. You need patience, high tolerance for frustration, scrupulous ethics and a tough skin.

Ch. Rallydon Beez Inmy Bonet, fifteen-inch bitch (Aus. & NZ Ch. Clarion Cloak ex Aus. Ch. Rallydon Sumthing Supa), owned by White Acres Kennels and Liz Rosbach, was Best in Sweepstakes at the 1995 Phoenix Arizona Specialty. She is linebred to Aus. Ch. Manahound Match Point, winner of the Australian National Beagle Council's Award of Merit, 1995, the highest honor bestowed on Beagles in Australia. *Kitten Rodwell*

If your bitch puppies are no better than their dam, or the dog puppies are no better than their sire, you have made no progress.

Keep only those puppies that are better than their sire or dam. By *better*, we mean better in one or two characteristics that you have decided to select for first. Remember that there is no point in selecting dogs that are inferior to the ones you already have. They can still be fun to show, but you will not have improved your line until the puppies you breed are better than their parents.

When you do get improvement, use these younger dogs as your next key breeders. Keep their parents in reserve in case you find that your new selections are producing some unsuspected and unfortunate results.

This brings up the question of whether you want to carry these defects along in your breeding program. If you decide that you do not, the answer is simply to not breed any affected dogs, their parents or their siblings. That, of course, is not an easy choice to make, because we are all so emotionally wrapped up in the good qualities of our dogs. This is where a thoroughly thought-out plan, such as the one recommended at the beginning of this section, will pay off.

If you decide to deal with a particular problem in your line, you might be able to eliminate it through selective breedings. These selective breedings are also called test breedings or progeny testing.

To improve your breeding stock, you must spend many hours researching your dogs' pedigrees. Not only should you ask questions about the dogs listed on the pedigree, but you should also ask about each of their siblings. It would be ideal if you could get all this information by making phone calls and writing letters to the owners, but the fact is that most breeder-owners are quite reluctant to give out information that they feel reflects badly on their dogs or their breeding program. Therefore, a good portion of the information will come in the form of gossip and hearsay and must be scrupulously filtered.

Start by making detailed notes on each dog in the pedigree(s) with which you are working. For our purposes, three generations are probablysufficient, provided you have full information. It is better to fill out information on these fourteen dogs than it is to have bits of information on other dogs in a six-generation pedigree. Gather as complete a picture on as many characteristics as possible on these dogs and their littermates as you can. You will need information on their conformation, inherited health problems and assets, temperament and whatever else will help you use the dogs to your advantage in a breeding program. You will usually find it easier to gather information on the sires, because the number of puppies they produce is much greater than that of the bitches.

Your next step is to do a pedigree analysis.

PEDIGREE ANALYSIS

Each animal in a pedigree can be analyzed phenotypically, based on the genetic nature revealed by physical characteristics and, to a certain extent, genotypically. This can become cumbersome with respect to paperwork, but it is essential to achieving your goal of stock improvement.

The fancy term "pedigree analysis" simply means an in-depth study of all of the dogs in your pedigrees and their siblings. You probably already know a great deal about the dogs in your pedigrees but have never thought of calling it pedigree analysis. That is just what it is. When you have asked questions and received answers about specific problems, the next step is to put this information into usable form.

As you gather information, look at the pedigrees in terms of your information instead of in terms of the dogs' names so you won't be influenced by a dog's record for high wins alone, which is sometimes, but not always, more an indication of the owner's status in the fancy than the actual quality of the dog or bitch.

To do an actual pedigree analysis, put your information in concise form on a card or individual evaluation sheet (see example). In addition to descriptive adjectives, you might add a placement as if the dog were in the ring and being judged against the ideal. Using the tail as an example, record this information:

Set: Okay (not perfect), somewhat low—second place

Brush: Good—first place

Length: Longer than desired—third place

The placement technique simplifies the process of choosing breeding partners. You want a breeding in which both dog and bitch don't have the same fault, at the same time allowing for acceptable levels of imperfection.

While looking at the pedigree, determine whether there is a pattern to the inheritance of the trait you are studying. In other words, does it come up in every generation, or does it skip a generation or more and show up again later? The rules for inheritance are that a dominant trait will *never* skip a generation but a recessive trait *may* not. Keep in mind that some of us have bred the same bad traits for so many generations that our recessive problems are beginning to appear like dominant traits.

OVERALL EVALUATION

If you are unable to determine the mode of inheritance (recessive or dominant), assume that the trait is recessive and work with the genetics for recessive traits.

Once you have gathered your information, several considerations are involved in making a breeding decision: what you have to work with (maybe deciding to start with new stock); how willing you are to cull your mistakes or, for that matter, to admit that you made a mistake and what tools you have available. Again, the tools are inbreeding, outcrossing and selection.

The next step is to inbreed or linebreed to the best animal available that presents the one or two qualities that are at the top of your list.

Inbreeding and its gentler partner linebreeding are the tools with which the dog breeder must work. Sadly, more fear is associated with them than any other facet of producing fine dogs.

Evaluation Sheet

Name: Height:

Owner: Weight:

Age: Parents:

Head   **Eye**   **Ear**
Skull: Color: Shape:
Muzzle: Haw: Placement:
Underjaw: Shape: Thickness:
Flews: Pigment: Length:

Teeth   **Neck**   **Expression**
Bite: Length:
Color: Thickness:
                            Throatiness:

Body   **Shoulder**   **Rear**
Topline: Angulation: Angulation:
Back length: Layback: Muscling:
Rib spring: Muscling: Width:
Chest depth: Hock/stifle:

Legs   **Feet**   **Tail**
Dewclaws: Cat's paw: Set:
Pasterns: Nail color: Brush:
Bone: Pad color: Length:
Wrist/growth: Pad thickness:
Elbow/chestline: Pad texture:

Coat   **Movement**   **Temperament**
Pigment: Front: Intelligence:
Texture: Rear: Trainability:
Length: Side:
Markings:

Homozygosity, the carrying of two of either the dominant or recessive genes of a pair of alleles, increases with more intense inbreeding regardless of how the genes express themselves phenotypically. Thus dominant, recessive, polygenic, qualitative or quantitative genes are more homozygous among more closely bred individuals. The increase in homozygosity is estimated from the inbreeding coefficient, a formula that can be found in any good book on genetics.

Inbred dogs, when bred to unrelated dogs, will tend to breed better than they look. On the other hand, outcrossed dogs tend to look better than they breed.

Inbreeding depression will occur eventually and cause loss of vigor and smaller litters with more puppies dying at an earlier age; the time at which this occurs differs among lines. Therefore, you can judge for yourself when to back off if you keep track of the coefficient of inbreeding for all your dogs. There is evidence from some studies that if inbreeding is continued, there will be a breakthrough, but most amateur/hobby breeders aren't tough enough to hold out this long.

There is a general feeling that inbreeding is dangerous and to be avoided and that linebreeding is totally safe. If you think about this in the light of our knowledge of genetics, it will be clear that this is illogical. Assuming that appropriate stock is available, whatever good can come of linebreeding will be obtained more quickly through inbreeding.

Inbreeding can be used to fix desirable genes; it does not create them. Nor does it create undesirable genes. The faults in the inbred animal are faults already in the line, and once identified, they can then be eliminated. This simply reduces the number of heterozygotes and increases the number of homozygotes.

We do not mean to imply that inbreeding is harmless. It should not be used by the uninformed or the inexperienced, and it should not be used by any breeder who cannot accept responsibility for the results and refuses to cull properly.

Outcrossing is a breeding method that has the least to recommend it. It is normally used to bring in new genetic material. The only time an outcross is indicated is when there is no dog in the particular line that carries or is likely to transmit the trait a breeder is seeking.

One of the reasons we don't like outcrossing is that, in one breeding, your puppies' carefully planned inheritance will be diluted by as much as half.

Another reason to avoid outcrossing is that you might, and probably will, open a Pandora's box of new genetic problems with which you will have to deal.

If you do choose to outcross, breed back to your line once the desired trait appears and work to maintain the qualities of your line as well as the

Ch. The Whim's Buckeye, thirteen-inch dog (Ch. Wandering Wind ex The Whim's Firecracker), owned by Mrs. A.C. Musladin, won ten Bests in Show; was Top Beagle, All Systems, 1971 and 1972; Top Hound, All Systems, 1972. He also distinguished himself as the sire of ninety-nine champions, including ten Top Producers.

new trait you outcrossed to get. It may take several generations to recoup from this one breeding. Be forewarned, however, that you may bring in new unwanted genes as well as the one you do want.

A better way to do this might be to breed to a dog that is the result of an outcross to your own line. In other words, half of that dog's pedigree includes your line.

If there is no such dog as just described, then you might outcross to a dog that is phenotypically similar to your dogs. The rationale for this is that if two dogs look alike, it took similar genes to make them that way. This, at least, gives you new genes without losing type.

There comes a time when you need to know whether your dogs are heterozygous for a particular trait. To eliminate a recessive gene, all the homozygous recessive individuals must be culled, as well as the affected individuals. This requires a breeding test.

It is an important point to understand that every animal derives 50 percent of its heritage from each parent, even though the contributions from each of the ancestors varies. The old theory that each parent contributes 50 percent, the grandparents 25 percent and the great-grandparents 12.5 percent has been disproved. The genes passed through the generations do not always occur in fixed percentages. There may even be ancestors who contribute little or no genes to the progeny due to independent assortment.

Progeny Testing

A recessive gene may skip not just one generation but several. If a dog or bitch is bred only a limited number of times, then you may never know whether that dog carries a particular gene. The most certain way to ascertain whether a dog carries the recessive gene in question is to breed that dog to a homozygous mate. Remember that only dogs who carry two recessive genes will show that trait. Therefore, it is unfair to blame only one of the parents when an undesirable trait appears.

Now, the formula for progeny testing is used for single gene inheritance, and most of the characteristics we are looking for are inherited in a more complex manner, but the formula should help guide you somewhat.

The easiest test for recessive genes is to mate the dog in question to one who already has the characteristic you suspect it may carry. In other words, breed your suspect dog that doesn't have the characteristic to a dog that does. This works whether the characteristic is desirable or detrimental.

Before you proceed with a breeding, decide how certain you want to be that your dog does or does not carry the gene so that you don't have to breed those dogs into their respective eternities. Mathematicians call this certainty "level of significance." For example, if you want to be 95 percent certain, this leaves only a 5 percent chance that your dog will produce without throwing any homozygous pups if it is a carrier. Please note that there is no such thing as 100 percent certainty. With this in mind, you can use the general formula for calculating how many puppies you need to give you 95 percent certainty that your dog is not a carrier. The formula follows:

$$S^n = P$$

S is the number of times your assumed carrier dog does not throw the recessive gene when bred to a homozygous dog. Thus, as an example,

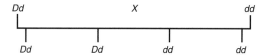

Don't panic! Read on!

In this case, half of the puppies will theoretically be carriers of the recessive gene but will be phenotypically normal, and the other half will be homozygous for the recessive gene and will manifest the trait. In other words, you can assign to the letter S the number 0.5 (half of the puppies).

Furthermore, *P* represents the probability that the dog will produce only puppies that are heterozygous for the trait, in spite of the fact that it carries the gene itself. This takes into consideration the fact that Beagles, being the sneaky little creatures that they are, might try this one on for a new trick. In our test case, we can be cautious and be 95 percent sure, and then *P* can equal 0.5; or we can be supercautious and be 99 percent sure, so *P* then equals 0.1.

The letter *n* represents the number of puppies your dog will have to produce to give you 95 percent or 99 percent assurance that the dog does not carry the factor.

The calculations for this formula will upset some of you, since *n* has been calculated by using logarithms. Don't despair! We have done the work for you. If you want to be 95 percent certain that your dog is not a carrier, then 4.3 puppies must be produced (5.0 puppies would be less messy). If you are of a conservative nature and want to be 99 percent certain, then 6.6 (7.0 puppies) will be necessary. If you are fortunate, you will get all seven puppies in your first litter. It will take two litters from this identical breeding for most of us.

DOMINANCE INHERITANCE

Oh, would that all our genetic problems and solutions were the result of single-gene inheritance!

The purpose of showing ratios is to give you an idea of what you might expect for any characteristic, good or bad, for which you think inheritance might be due to a single gene.

To illustrate single-gene inheritance, we will use von Willebrand's Disease (vWD). Although there have not been many documented cases in Beagles, there have been some, and since most most breeders do not test for the problem, there is a chance the disease is increasing and will be a greater problem for the breed in the future.

Von Willebrand's Disease is the result of abnormalities in the blood-clotting system. One of the factors involved is the reduced activity of Factor VII, and one of the symptoms is a slow clotting time when a nail has been cut too far back into the quick. If clotting does not take place within two or five minutes, there might be reason for concern, and a subsequent test should be made by your veterinarian's reference laboratory. For some reason, the disease will improve with age and is associated with hypothyroidism. This disease seems to have a great deal of variability, possibly due to modifying genes.

The genetics for von Willebrand's Disease have already been worked out. Normal to normal produces no affected pups, and every dog that has the disease had at least one affected parent. When an affected dog was bred to an unaffected dog, the ratios of affected to unaffected was approximately 1:1—the ratio expected for a dominant gene. Therefore, von Willebrand's Disease is due to a dominant gene.

Using Punnett's Square to illustrate the products of a mating of an affected dog *(Vv)* to an unaffected dog *(vv)*, the results would be

	v	v
V	Vv	Vv
v	vv	vv

You can see from this illustration that 50 percent of the puppies will be affected. The unaffected puppies do not carry the gene at all, since the dominant gene will always manifest itself.

An incomplete dominant is a variation that manifests itself in the heterozygote. Instead of full expression when even one gene is present, the heterozygote falls somewhere in-between. Hypothyroidism is an example of incomplete dominance in Beagles, but the most graphic illustration is in flowers.

In four-o'clock plants, when a pure line with red petals is crossed with a pure line of white-petaled flowers, the result is not red, as expected, but pink! The explanation is that the red gene is incompletely dominant over the white gene. In fact, the key to identifying an incomplete dominant is the phenotype that falls between the dominant and the recessive phenotype.

RECESSIVE INHERITANCE

To refresh your memory, it takes two genes, one from the father and one from the mother, to produce a characteristic that is inherited recessively. There are not many characteristics in the Beagle that have this inheritance, so to illustrate it, we will have to borrow from some other breeds and use cleft palates as an example. You could replace cleft palates with epilepsy, if you believe our anecdotal evidence that epilepsy can be followed as a simple recessive.

Again, you can use Punnett's Square to show what the expected ratios will be if two dogs are mated, both of which carry the gene *(c)* for cleft palate *(cc)* but are themselves normal in appearance. They should produce three normal (two carriers) and one affected.

	C	c
C	CC	Cc
c	Cc	cc

This follows the normal 3:1 phenotype with 1:2:1 genotype. When you are dealing with genetic traits, the first step is to decide how they are inherited. Are you dealing with a single pair of genes, or is more than one pair involved? Is the trait you want dominant or recessive? Has the trait's mode of inheritance been worked out, or must you try to do this yourself?

To determine whether a trait is dominant or recessive, you should know that dominant factors never skip a generation. Once a dominant factor disappears, it is gone forever unless it is reintroduced from outside. The puppies that exhibit the trait, whether they are homozygous or heterozygous, carry the gene. If we are dealing with a single pair of genes and a dog exhibits the dominant trait but does not reproduce it in every puppy, we know he is heterozygous for that trait.

Bayard Cat And Mouse With Tragband (Ch. Dialynne Tolliver of Tragband ex Bayard Misty Cat), pictured at six months of age with owner Andrew Brace. She won Best Puppy in Show at her first show, the Scottish National Specialty. *Carol Ann Johnson*

POLYGENIC TRAITS

Most of the desirable characteristics that we seek, such as good shoulder layback, correct movement and good temperament, are the result of many genes, with other factors influencing their expression. Some of the other influences are incomplete penetrance, the presence of modifying genes or poor environmental conditions.

Polygenic traits result from the cumulative effect of a number of different genes. Different traits probably have different numbers of genes involved. They can mimic either recessive or dominant inheritance and therefore create incorect conclusions. This is also complicated by the fact that polygenic traits are especially subject to environmental influences.

More traits are polygenic than are controlled by a single gene pair. The problem is that some traits that are desirable are desirable in the heterozygous state. When this is the case, no matter how hard you try to "fix" the trait by breeding correct individual to individual, you will still get some dogs (even after many generations of selective breeding) that do not have the desired trait.

For example, the genetic makeup that produces the correct shoulder will not breed true. No matter how many generations of correct shoulders are in your pedigrees, there will continue to be individuals that will have a short upper arm to go with well-laid-back shoulders, or a long upper arm with a steep shoulder.

Even if knowledge of certain hybrid traits doesn't exactly speed you to your goals, at least you know that certain "failures" go with the territory. But don't relax vigilance in selecting for desirable traits that experience has shown do not breed true.

Temperament is another trait that cannot be "fixed" in dogs. *Fixed* means that generations of selected breeding have been conducted so that an entire population or strain has the identical genetic makeup and breeds true for the trait, generation after generation.

The proper combination of intenseness, stubborness, independence, sense of humor and pack cooperativeness are contradictory characteristics.

Recessive traits, whether simple or polygenic, are difficult to eliminate from the population. These pesky traits get into a population, usually through a top-producing stud dog, and before anyone realizes there is a problem, anywhere from 20 percent to 90 percent of the breed's population are carriers.

Eliminating affected individuals with a dominant trait will reduce the incidence to zero in one generation. Eliminating affected individuals with a recessive or polygenic trait will *never* reduce the incidence to zero, and it might take as many as fifty generations to get the incidence below 1 percent, depending on how high the carrier rate was originally.

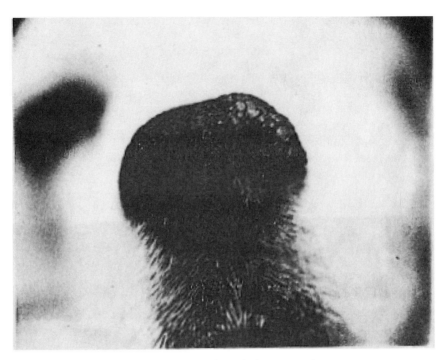

Dry left nostril in Beagle with dry-eye syndrome.

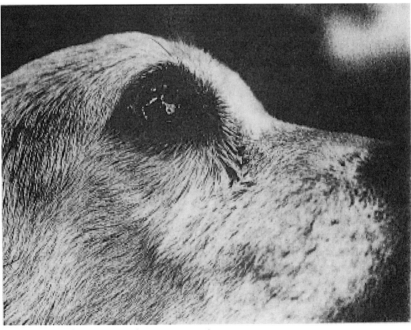

Prominent right eye secondary to acute glaucoma.

chapter 16

Your Beagle's Health and Genetics

SEE NO EVIL

Compared to humans, dogs have poor close-up vision, less focusing ability and are relatively colorblind. Evidence as cited in *DVM*, March 1986, indicates that dogs may see the color red. Their pupils, however, give them superior peripheral vision and night vision.

The Beagle, though relatively free of many of the major genetic eye problems afflicting other breeds, does have its own set of difficulties.

Cherry Eye

Your promising three-month-old puppy suddenly develops a small, red cherry-like swelling in the inner corner of the lower lid. Ugly! What is it?

Definition: This condition is simply an enlargement of the gland of the third eyelid with resultant prolapse. It is thought to be due to inflammation and/or a lack of connective tissue bands that hold the gland in place. It is unsightly but probably does not bother the dog much.

This small gland provides about 30 percent of the aqueous portion of the tear film, so surgical removal, which in the past was the treatment, leaves the dog more susceptible to developing dry eye syndrome (q.v.) if the remainder of tear production is compromised.

The incidence of cherry eye in the current conformation Beagle population is significant. Occasionally, an entire litter is affected. Not enough data have been reported to date to determine the mode of transmission. There is some indication that it functions as a simple recessive.

Management: Occasionally, the simple application of an ophthalmic ointment containing both an antibiotic and a potent steroid will reduce the gland's

Lil' Sis, adult Beagle with severe chondrodystrophy. Note the shortened neck, curved back and deformed front and rear legs. *Diane Quenell*

Lil' Sis in frontal view. Note the position of the fore-legs. *Diane Quenell*

size. Recurrence is possible, however. If the protrusion persists, the gland should be sutured back in place by your veterinarian. When properly done (and it is not always easy!), the gland remains intact, and your little Beagle regains its pretty expression.

Under no circumstances should the gland be totally removed, unless it is affected by cancer, which is rare.

Dry-Eye Syndrome (Keratoconjunctivits Sicca)

One of your Beagle's normally bright, shiny eyes suddenly appears dry and lusterless. In the mornings, a thick, stringy discharge accumulates over the eyeball. Several days or weeks later, that eye, if not treated, is red, squinty and very painful.

This is a serious disease. Painful for the Beagle, KCS can result in severe ulceration and scarring of the cornea and blindness and may eventually require removal of the eyeball.

Cause: Drying of the cornea results from inadequate tear production. Tear glands may be defective as a result of severe system infection, such as canine parvovirus or canine distemper. Surgical removal of the third eyelid gland may be at fault. Some oral sulfa medications have triggered KCS.

If the nerves to the tear glands are not functioning properly, the Beagle may also have a dry nostril on the affected side. A young Beagle with a dry nostril should be watched closely for the first indication of dry eye.

Plugged tear ducts can cause dry eye, but the preceding two factors are the most common mechanisms in Beagles.

Reports indicate that occasionally, dogs with dry eye may have a hypothyroid condition. Although thyroid supplementation does not increase tear production, it has been shown to improve the health of the eye tissues. Thus, all dogs with dry eye should be tested for a defective thyroid function.[1]

It has also been reported that KCS can be an autoimmune disease that manifests itself as an adverse reaction to the dog's own tear glands. Successful experimental treatment has consisted of cyclosporin drops as an immunosuppressant.

Diagnosis: Run, don't walk, to your nearest veterinary ophthalmologist (eye specialist). A paper-strip test (known as the *Schirmer test*) indicating reduced tear flow confirms the diagnosis.

Treatment: Your veterinarian will try to find the underlying causes while placing the Beagle on a regimen of eyedrops and ointments to lubricate the eye and prevent infection and inflammation, along with oral medication to

---

[1]Brightman, Alan. *Washington State University Animal Health Notice, 9:1, 1987.*

stimulate tear production. Transplanting a salivary-gland duct to drain into the eye works well when medicating the eye alone is insufficient.

In those Beagles we have followed for years, fluctuations in the production of tears occur. As a result, frequency of administration of treatment agents needs to be adjusted from time to time.

Of course, any underlying disease, such as hypothyroidism, requires treatment as well.

Glaucoma

Definition: Glaucoma is an eye problem that researchers have found Beagles, among other breeds, prone to develop. It results when the normal fluids within the eyeball fail to drain normally back into the bloodstream. When this happens, too much pressure builds up in the eye. The pressure increases to above normal levels and can eventually cause damage to the optic nerve. The condition seems to show up more in older dogs.

Symptoms and signs: Signs of glaucoma can appear gradually or abruptly. As pressure builds up, the retina and optic nerve are compromised, eventually leading to blindness.

Chronic glaucoma is not always easy to recognize, and usually one must use an instrument called a tonometer to measure the intraocular pressure. Other clues are changes in the eye's appearance and possibly the dog's behavior.

Signs of glaucoma include discomfort, tearing, inflammation of the sclera (white) of the eye, a cloudy cornea and enlargement of the eyeball. Left untreated, an eye with glaucoma may eventually bulge to the point where the eyelids can no longer close over the eye. This can cause the cornea to dry out and ulcerate, making surgical removal of the eye necessary.

Treatment: In many cases, medical treatment is possible. Your veterinarian may be able to decrease the fluid production and increase drainage with medication.

Because the exact dosage of medication is a delicate balance, the dog may have to be hospitalized for several days. After that, the owner must treat the dog scrupulously for the medication to be effective. Rechecks with the veterinarian, of course, are a requirement.

Most cases of glaucoma cannot be treated medically forever, and surgery may become necessary to control the disease. Several techniques are available, and if you have access to a board-certified ophthalmologist, one of the techniques can be employed.

Cyclocryosurgery is one method; here, the eye's fluid-producing tissue is frozen to eliminate future pressure buildup. Another method is to evacuate a blind eyeball and insert a prosthesis, making the eye look fairly normal. Sometimes the eyeball is simply removed.

Nothing can be done to prevent glaucoma. However, one study showed that prophylactic treatment of glaucoma in one eye may delay the onset in the other eye (bilateral glaucoma). Several breeds were studied. Beagles, among others, were shown to have a significantly higher risk of developing the condition than other breeds.

It is generally accepted that glaucoma is hereditary, since it is prevalent in certain breeds like the Beagle. However, unlike other breeds, Beagles respond well to prophylactic treatment such as timolol, dichlorphenamide and/or echothiophate to delay the development of glaucoma in the second eye. The average time lengthened from five months to ten months.

Although glaucoma is generally considered to be bilateral, it does not necessarily develop clinically into a bilateral condition.

In the Beagle, glaucoma is inherited as an autosomal recessive trait. To date in the conformation Beagle population, one line has reported seven cases of glaucoma: four in the offspring of one bitch and three from a daughter of this bitch. In all these cases, a weakness of the tissue holding the lens in place was the causative agent.

White Haws

Dogs have three eyelids: an upper, a lower and a third (or nictitating membrane). Constructed of elastic cartilage covered by conjunctiva, the third eyelid is located where the upper and lower lids converge at the inner corner of the eye. This eyelid protects the eye in a fashion similar to the other two eyelids, but it also acts as a wiper to remove pollen, dust and other irritants from the eye. This membrane also contains an important tear gland in dogs.

The third eyelid's main portion is covered by a pink-colored mucous membrane, usually showing a dark brown edge where it is visible. This pigmentation is considered normal. On occasion, the brown edge is only lightly pigmented, and appears almost white. It is not a serious problem, but contrasting with the iris, it gives a less than pleasant expression. The condition may be present on one or both sides and is not an anatomical deformity but is genetic in origin.

Cataracts

A cataract is an opacity of the lens of the eye, usually apparent on inspection of the naked eye as a dull whiteness of the pupil. Vision decreases gradually as the cataract progresses.

Cataracts are classified by several methods. Some are acquired as a result of trauma. Some are congenital and are present at birth, and sometimes they are classified by position.

Although it is unusual for cataracts to be other than bilateral, chondrodystrophic Beagles frequently develop an early cataract in the left eye.

The two types of cataracts associated with Beagles are senior cataracts and juvenile cataracts. Senior cataracts appear as the dog ages, and literature suggests that almost every dog over the age of eight years will develop some degree of cataract. Juvenile cataracts have now been reported in Beagles and are defined as any cataract that appears before the age of six years.

Dogs can accommodate very well to a slow loss of vision if their environment remains unchanged. Cataracts can be surgically treated by removal of the lens, and lens transplants, which have worked so well in people, are now available for dogs.

The scientific community agrees on the hereditary nature of cataracts, but how they are inherited is still unclear. This is probably due to the existence of different kinds of cataracts and the various reasons for their development.

HYPOTHYROIDISM

Since the incidence of hypothyroidism (low thyroid function) is on the increase in Beagles, as well as the general dog population, this section is particularly detailed.

Hypothyroidism is a generalized metabolic disease resulting from a deficiency of the thyroid hormones tetraiodothyronine or thyroxine (T_4) and/ or triodothyroxine (T_3).

The disease develops gradually after puberty, and typical signs tend to occur in midlife. In nearly 90 percent of cases, the cause of canine hypothyroidism is autoimmune thyroiditis (like Hashimoto's disease in humans); the remaining 10 percent have thyroid atrophy of a unknown cause.

Sometimes, a transient thyroid problem occurs in conjunction with another disease or secondary to use of a drug being given to treat another condition. This problem will clear up if the thyroid function has not been suppressed too long.

Physiology: The thyroid gland is located just below the voice box on either side of the trachea. The thyroid works like a thermostat, and its three principal functions are (1) to ensure that body cells take up and burn oxygen effectively, (2) to generate enough heat to enable body cells to maintain proper temperature and (3) to maintain metabolic activity. Thyroid hormones either alone or in conjunction with other hormones are involved in protein, fat and carbohydrate metabolism; growth and maturation; normal libido and reproduction and normal skin functions.

The messenger that regulates how high (or low) the thermostat is to be set is a protein called thyroid stimulating hormone (TSH), which originates in the brain. TSH works directly on the thyroid gland to produce two types of thyroglobulin: a lot of fT_4 (free T_4) and a small amount of fT_3 (free T_3). T_4 and T_3 must travel to every cell in the body to regulate metabolism.

Most T_4 and T_3 thyroglobulins have an escort and are bound to other proteins. TT_4 and TT_3 are total thyroglobulin as measured in a blood sample, whereas fT_4 and fT_3 are active forms because they are unattached. These active forms play an important role when measuring the overall health of the thyroid gland. The protein-bound T_4 and T_3 are held in storage (in the blood) until they are needed.

Recently thyroglobulin antibodies to T_4 and T_3 (T_{4A} and T_{3A}) have been identified. These antibodies are not the good guys, because they attack your Beagle's own tissues. This is called an autoimmune response. The tendency for antibodies to get out of control is usually genetic.

Signs and symptoms: If your Beagle is not producing enough thyroid hormones, a variety of physical problems can occur. The ones most common to the Beagle are weight gain; dry, sparse coat; skin infections and flea allergy; food allergies; smelly ears due to excessive wax production and ear infections that are difficult to clear; dry-eye syndrome; a bleeding tendency (for example, being slow to clot after cutting the quick of a toenail) and reproduction problems, such as infertility, low sperm count in the male and infrequent seasons in the female.

Diagnosis: Although a screening for T_4 can be used as an initial test to eliminate any young dogs that fall below the normal range, we now know that a single T_4 test is wholly incomplete and could be misleading. Today's Beagle breeder needs to run a complete set of thyroid levels.

In August 1996, the American Kennel Club and the University of California/Davis held a sypmosium on the UC-Davis campus to discuss canine hypothyroidism. At this symposium, a practical guide to diagnosing and monitoring the disease was established. For all dogs, an initial database should be established consisting of a case history, physical examination, complete blood count, blood chemistry panel and urinalysis.

The workup for any dog we are considering for breeding should include total T_4 (TT_4), free T_4 measured by equilibrium dialysis (fT_4ed), thyroglobulin autoantibodies (TgAA) and canine thyroid stimulating hormone (cTSH). TSH levels are not essential if the dog is normal on all other parts of the thyroid tests.

Test	Range	Ideal
TT_4	22–54	38
TT_3	1.2–3.1	>2.2
fT_4	12–39	>25
fT_3	2.2–4.8	>3.5
T_{4A}	<25	<10
T_{3A}	<10	<5

Bitches should be tested after their first season, and males should be tested at ten to fourteen months. Although mid-range is adequate for adult Beagles, young dogs should have baseline levels in the upper half of the adult normal ranges.

A Beagle with no clinical signs and symptoms of hypothyroidism and normal test results can be used for breeding. If there is a family history of hypothyroidism, the tests should be repeated annually.

On the other hand, a dog with normal results that shows clinical signs of hypothyroidism should be withheld from breeding and retested in two to six months. If the dog's health appears to be normal, but the test results are abnormal, the experts again recommend waiting and retesting in two to six months. Abnormal results with clinical signs and symptoms warrant treatment and a hold on breeding.

Treatment: Beagles respond well to twice-daily treatment with L-thyroxine. It is important to split the total daily requirement into two portions, because the half-life of the hormone is very short in the dog, lasting only ten to twelve hours, compared to a duration of several days in humans.

Once treated adequately, the dog's prognosis is excellent.

Regular monitoring once or twice yearly is needed to ensure that treatment dosages are proper to maintain thyroid levels within the upper half of the normal range. It is recommended that a TT_4 or fT_4ed test be conducted four to six hours after thyroid supplementation. The test result, known as the "peak value," should be within the high-normal to slightly high range. Although generic drugs are usually quite satisfactory for most medical problems, they do not seem to work as well in dogs with a thyroid deficiency (in contrast to humans), so treatment should be with a name-brand, synthetic levothyroxine sodium product.

If your Beagle is diagnosed as hypothyroid, it will probably be on medication for the rest of its life. Dosage may need to be readjusted from time to time or in a few cases actually eliminated—hence the need for annual testing. Fortunately, in spite of the many areas of the body this disease can affect, with treatment, the lifespan of the dog is usually not affected.

Further comments: In addition to an apparent genetic predisposition, nutritional factors, viral infections and immunologic mechanisms may play a role.

Thyroid deficiency also plays a role in bone marrow hypoplasia (decreased or failed blood-cell formation) associated with immune-mediated blood diseases and also increases the risks of von Willebrand's disease (see the "Dominance Inheritance" section in Chapter 15, "Genetics: How Can I Use What I Don't Understand?").

Although it is not always possible to determine the exact cause of the condition, hypothyroidism is most often the result of autoimmune destruction, where the affected animal's body is forming antibodies against its own tissues. In these cases, the thyroid is destroyed, and as a result, thyroid hormones are no longer produced.

Several environmental factors have been implicated in triggering autoimmune diseases, thyroid disease in particular, in both humans and other animals. These include retrovirus and parvovirus infections, use of certain drugs or toxicants, increased pollution and use of pesticides, nutritional imbalances and our penchant for over-vaccinating.

The incidence of hypothyroidism in Beagles is on the rise. The hereditary nature of this disease has been established in humans and dogs, although it appears to be the predisposition to develop thyroid disease that is inherited.

Although every case would have to be biopsied to be proven, Dr. Jean Dodds and others have come to the conclusion that this disease is inherited as an incomplete dominant. Also keep in mind that this disease sometimes doesn't show up until middle age after the dog may have been used as breeding stock.

PROBLEMS WITH THE REPRODUCTIVE SYSTEM

Intersex

> *You are trimming the excess hair around the rump of your eight-month-old Beagle bitch, preparatory to a show. Suddenly, you notice for the first time a growth protruding from the vulva. Upon closer examination, it seems to resemble the tip of a penis! How can this be? Why, your bitch even had her first season the month before.*

Definition: An *intersex* is an animal or person who has the internal reproductive organs (ovaries and testes) of both sexes. This condition, formerly known as hermaphroditism, is to be differentiated from pseudohermaphroditism, which is the presence of external genitalia of one sex and the internal gonads of the other. This latter condition is thought to be a congenital defect (a noninheritable abnormality that occurs in utero while the embryo is developing) due to some noxious influence during pregnancy—drugs, toxins and so on. An enlarged clitoris may result, giving the appearance of male genitalia in a female.

Developmentally, the normal fetus begins as a female with differentiation into a male occurring as a result of male-determining genes. The rudimentary female reproductive tract is replaced by the developing male reproductive system. If there is a disruption in this normal process, an intersex results.

Occurrence in Beagles: To date, in the current families of conformation Beagles, eight apparent females have been diagnosed as intersex, and there is a report of one male with malformed external male genitalia.

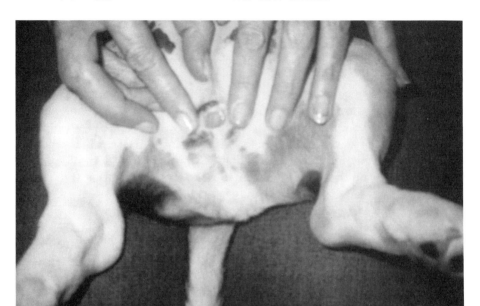

A four-month-old Beagle puppy showing an enlarged clitoris protruding from the vagina. Laboratory studies and subsequent spaying confirmed the diagnosis of intersex.

One Beagle, a newborn, had a normal-appearing vagina and an enlarged clitoris that resembled a penis; it was put down. Another intersex Beagle was discovered when an attempted breeding was unsuccessful and the examining veterinarian found an enlarged clitoris obstructing the vaginal canal. A third intersex was diagnosed at twelve weeks, and five more were diagnosed between four-and-a-half and eight months of age. Each affected Beagle was from a different litter. Six, however, had one common ancestor within a few generations. There is one deceased male common to all these pedigrees. The other two were from unrelated families—one conformation, one not.

Genetics of intersex: A genetic study[2] was done on a family of American Cocker Spaniels in which nine true intersex and two XXY males (males with two female sex chromosomes) occurred in ten separate but related litters.

---

[2]*J.R. Selden et al. "Inherited XX Sex Reversal in the Cocker Spaniel Dog," Human Genetics 67 (1984):62-69.*

Eight of the females also had enlarged clitores.

The parents of these litters were related within a few generations through at least one common denominator. All were related to one deceased male ancestor. Cellular, serological, anatomical and genetic studies were done, with the conclusion that transmission is most likely through the mode of an autosomal recessive gene, originally a mutant.

No studies have been published on Beagles to date, but most likely the transmission is the same for our breed.

Management: First, a correct diagnosis must be made to differentiate between a true intersex and a pseudohermaphrodite. A fasting blood level of testosterone, the male hormone, is compared with the level following injection of human chorionic gonadotropin, a hormone that stimulates the testes to produce testosterone. The normal female will have some testosterone in the blood. However, if testicular tissue is present, there may be a marked rise in the level of testosterone after the injection of human chorionic gonadotropin.

If this study proves your Beagle to be a true intersex, it should then be spayed. The enlarged clitoris may recede somewhat, or it may be removed if it protrudes so far that infection or injury is likely.

If, on the other hand, your Beagle proves to be a pseudohermaphrodite, then a careful review of the management of the dam's pregnancy is in order. Special attention needs to be given as to whether and what kinds of antibiotics or other drugs were used at the time of breeding and early in pregnancy, as well as whether the Beagle was exposed to toxins, sprays and so on.

Unfortunately, no test is available outside research centers to check for carrier status in the siblings. Natural selection will play a part. Not all females are bred, and though there are reports of litters born to intersex dogs, these are obviously rare.

Sterility in the Male Beagle

Over the past twenty to thirty years, several incidents of sterility in male Beagles have occurred. There is suggestive evidence that this condition may be inherited. If it is, obviously it will be self-limiting; we won't have to worry about it any more. Some lines report a higher proportion of sterile males than others, but this may be a function of varying practices of reporting among Beagle breeders.

It is heartbreaking to discover that a promising stud has stopped producing viable sperm.

The typical history involves a young dog that had sired one to three litters and then became infertile. Extensive work-ups at diagnostic centers in several cases failed to account for the arrest of spermatogenesis (sperm formation). Some of these Beagles have had decreased levels of circulating thyroxine, the hormone produced by the thyroid gland, but thyroid supplementation did not restore fertility.

Suggested causative factors include hypothyroidism, a chronic low-grade infection of the prostate gland and immune-related problems. These are in addition to obvious causes, such as brucellosis or an acute infection of the testes.

A temporary drop in fertility may occur with stress, particular medications or a severe illness from which the dog recovers. In these cases, sperm production will return.

Not enough data are available to date to draw any conclusions. The condition has been known to occur in all breeds and continues to be a puzzle.

My (JM) personal hunch is that some lines may be more prone to immune-deficient problems, with specific target organs determined genetically. In this case, the target organs would be the testes.

Undescended Testicle

Monorchidism, the failure of one testicle to descend into the scrotum (the external sac that holds the testicles), is a commonly reported phenomenon in Beagles. Cryptorchidism, the failure of both to descend, is rare.

In most dogs, testicles normally descend into the scrotum before birth. In Beagles, frequently this does not occur until after birth. Sometimes testicles are difficult to feel because they are so small. A testicle that moves up and down from groin to scrotum is not unusual. Puppies can also retract them in play or when cold or frightened. So don't worry if your pup's testicles behave like a yo-yo.

The typical breeder heaves a sigh of relief if both little testicles are neatly in place by six to eight weeks of age. If you have a particularly promising male puppy with an undescended testicle still at twelve weeks, don't give up on him. We have seen the second come down nicely at between four and five months of age. One nice male dropped his at eight months, with full development of the testicle by ten months.

If the testicle can be felt in the groin but does not move, a short cord is the most likely cause. Some breeders report that *gentle* regular stretching of the cord and testicle while the pup lies on its back will lengthen the cord. Others have achieved success with a course of hormone injections prescribed by their veterinarians. It may be that these testicles simply needed a bit more time to descend.

A late-descending testicle does not appear to affect fertility in the adult Beagle.

Because monorchidism is an inherited condition, the adult Beagle with only one descended testicle should never be used for breeding. Your veterinarian should be consulted about the advisability of castration (surgical removal of both testicles) in these cases.

DEM BONES

Hip Dysplasia

Hip dysplasia (HD) is a defect of the hip joint—more specifically, a failure of the head of the femur to fit properly into the acetabulum (socket of the hip joint). If the fit is not correct, probably secondary to capsular and ligamentous laxity, the head of the femur undergoes abnormal stress that eventually results in degenerative osteoarthitis and crippling.

Reports of HD in Beagles is increasing in direct relationship to the increase of breeders having their dogs tested; more dogs are being x-rayed, and consequently, more cases are being reported. It leaves us with the feeling that the breed is far more affected than we have been willing to admit in the past.

Signs and symptoms: A stilted gait, lameness, discomfort on rising, unwillingness to jump or put weight on the hind legs and "bunny hopping" are all signs that your Beagle *might* be dysplastic. The only way to be sure whether your Beagle is dysplastic or clear is to have it tested by a veterinarian qualified in reading the x-ray results.

Diagnosis: The most common form of testing to date is by x-ray. A new technique called PennHip from the University of Pennsylvania Veterinary School is now available and can be performed on young puppies. This procedure determines the degree of capsular laxity and, with follow-up studies, can offer an index to the development of the mature joint and the probability of degenerative change.

The PennHip examination can be performed only by a specially-trained and certified veterinarian. A breeder who wants to avail himself of this procedure can be referred to such a veterinarian by contacting the University of Pennsylvania.

Treatment: In Beagles, the primary method of treatment is watchful waiting. Most affected Beagles don't become severe enough for owners to consider euthanasia. Pain can be dealt with by the use of various anti-inflammatory medications. A rather sophisticated and expensive operative procedure is available, but Beagles don't seem to suffer sufficiently for owners to have routinely opted for this treatment.

Genetics: The great volume of evidence clearly points to HD being a polygenic trait with the actual manifestation determined by a combination of genetic and environmental factors.

An outcropping of the University of Pennsylvania study was the information that the x-ray technique required by the Orthopedic Foundation of America (OFA) produces about 24 percent false negatives (these dogs could be OFA-evaluated as clear). This might be an explanation for why so many studies and breeder efforts to breed clear-to-clear have not been as rewarding as expected.

Chondrodystrophy or "the Funnies"

Your litter has arrived. The smallest pup seems slow to nurse and less vigorous than its siblings. Supplemental feeding is needed, and soon you must contend with diarrhea as well. After a week or ten days of fluid supplementation and antibiotics, your pup seems to be catching up and is nursing along with the rest. Development seems to be normal. Up on its feet by three weeks, it is hiking around the whelping box. One night, it starts to scream and is unable to put weight on one of its forelegs. You assume that it twisted its leg somehow and try to make it comfortable. Within a day or two, all seems well. But not so!

By about four weeks, it seems to be having difficulty getting up on its feet and moves with a shuffling gait. Plucky, very responsive and affectionate, the puppy becomes special. Visits to your veterinarian, treatments of various kinds and a variety of diagnoses become the story of this pup's early weeks.

Reaching four to six months of age, your pup seems completely comfortable, and the condition has stabilized. At this point, your pup is small, has crooked front legs, a roach to his back, walks with a limp and shows weak and cow-hocked rear quarters. Skin is frequently itchy, and your pup will rub its back just above the tail on whatever is available. Intelligent, affectionate and less active than the usual, your pup makes a marvelous companion.

Definition: Chondrodystrophy, or multiple epiphyseal dysplasia, as it has been known in the veterinary literature, is a disease affecting the long bones and vertebral bodies in which there is pathological enchondral growth. This means that there is a failure in the growth centers within the cartilage precursors and bones, resulting in stunted, twisted limbs and shortened, deformed vertebrae, the latter producing signs associated with intervertebral disc disease.

Some dog breeds are typically achondroplastic and are characterized as disproportionate dwarfs. Members of this group are the Pekingese, Basset Hound, Dachshund and, to a lesser extent, the Boston Terrier and Cavalier King Charles Spaniel. The Beagle, too, is considered basically as belonging in this general category. Most likely, as the forebearers of the modern Beagle were bred down in size to function more efficiently with rabbits and hares, certain genetic traits were incorporated that predispose the breed to achondroplastic characteristics—short legs, large head, crooked front extremities and so on.

Genetics: An autosomal recessive mode of transmission is cited in the available veterinary literature. More likely, it is more complicated than that. As with any genetic predisposition, extrauterine influences such as illness, nutrition, drugs, toxins and so on may determine the severity of the process in the developing puppies. You therefore can see pups that are so severely affected that they die, as well as pups that are only mildly affected.

The principle of multiplicity of genetic defects seems to apply to these pups. Often seen in conjunction with this condition are the failure to thrive, bad bites, a predisposition to dental disease, an early left-eye cataract, increased vulnerability to infection, short toes and, in one instance, a hypoplastic (underdeveloped) lung.

Diagnosis: In addition to the clinical signs mentioned already, x-rays in the early stages (about three weeks of age) reveal abnormal epiphyseal ossification centers (the bony growth centers at the ends of the long bones and in the vertebral bodies) in some or all of the limb bones and vertebrae. At six to eight weeks, the best age to make the diagnosis, the growth centers are mottled and frayed with some irregular spots of calcification present. By six months of age, these changes have disappeared, and the growth centers are incorporated into the bone. At this point, the degenerative osteoarthritic changes that have developed in the joints obscure the original disease process and are most frequently seen in the shoulder, elbow and hip joints. Hip dysplasia as well as disc disease can be common sequelae.

Another consistent finding in these puppies is the absence of frontal sinuses noted on lateral x-rays of the skull. James Ticer, DVM, Veterinary Radiologist, cites this as evidence of probable interbreeding with a Toy breed at some point in the Beagle's evolution. Pictures of Queen Elizabeth I's "pocket Beagles" show an apple-headed, short-muzzled tiny hound. Was this when it happened?

Occurrence in Beagles: Over the last thirty-two years, sixty-one Beagles with pedigrees have been reported to us, along with verbal reports of others without specific identification, that most likely had or have chondrodystrophy.

It was only during the 1987 to 1988 period that a diagnosis of these "funnies," as they are affectionately known, was made. These cases range in severity from a fourteen-day-old puppy that had to be put down for failure to thrive and inability to move around to a mildly affected five-year-old that has a slight roach and a rearquarter limp. Varying degrees of involvement lie between these extremes.

Generally, one affected pup may appear in a litter; however, in one litter we know of, three were affected. Repeat breedings have produced normal puppies. In our kennel, the pattern is one in which the C-6 and L-7 vertebrae seem especially targeted. We would suspect that it varies from line to line.

Management: Obviously, those Beagles that survive to a comfortable adult life should be neutered or spayed. Because they are especially bright and responsive, probably due to the extra handling and care required during their first few months of life, they make wonderful companions. So affliction does not automatically bode euthanasia. Normal siblings may well be carriers. If

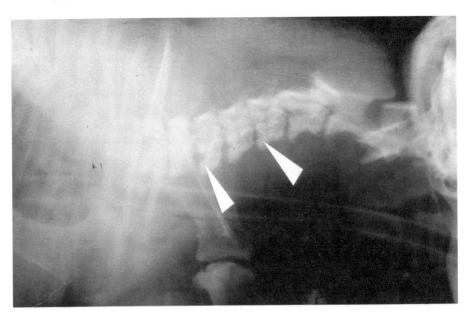

Cervical spine radiograph of Lil' Sis, taken at nine months of age. Note the erosion of the endplates of the vertebral bodies and joint changes in the upper cervical spine.

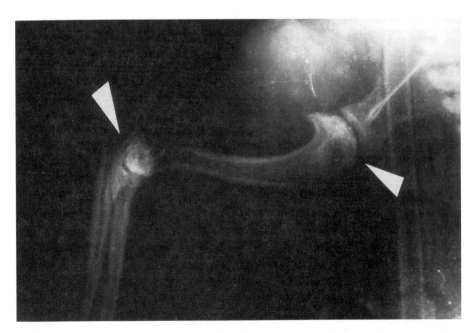

A radiograph of shoulder and elbow joints, Lil' Sis at nine months of age. Note the irregularity of the joint surface of the upper arm, spotty densities and bony erosion. Similar changes are present in the elbow joint.

bred, care should be taken to find partners from a family free of chondrodystrophy. Even then, an affected puppy may turn up, because this is obviously a trait bred into the Beagle's genetic history.

It is important to recognize chondrodystrophic puppies, because misdiagnosis can be terribly discouraging. For the first twenty-five years, those cases produced in our kennel were variously diagnosed as having vitamin D deficiency, septicemia of the newborn or injury to one or more of the joints; a variety of treatments was advised.

Pain relief (aspirin works nicely) and protection from injury can see the plucky little ones through the acute phase of the process. Their life span is no different from that of the uninvolved Beagles.

Slipped Kneecap

Any leg problem is generally a subject that is carefully ignored or considered unimportant by breeders. Not so! It is very important, and information regarding it is rarely passed on to novice breeders or owners.

Definition: The common name for this disorder is "slipping" or "slipped stifles," resulting from either subluxation (partial dislocation) or complete dislocation of the patella or kneecap.

Slipped kneecaps are seen more often in small dogs than large ones. In the dog, intermittent or recurrent subluxations are characterized by the animal appearing normal one minute and holding up a hind limb the next. The dog generally does not appear in pain and does not resist any effort to examine the affected limb.

Subluxation usually is mesial—toward the midline of the body—with the stifle adducted (pulled or drawn to the midline) and the hock rotated outward. Lateral displacement is infrequent and usually the result of severe trauma. Bilateral involvement is rare and is evidenced by difficulty standing and walking in a hopping manner.

Treatment: In all cases, surgical repair consisting of ligament and tendon repair is indicated.

Genetics: Genetically speaking, we don't have enough pedigrees to form an opinion regarding the nature of this condition's heritability, but since there seems to be a tendency for certain Beagle families to have had more than one example in the show ring over the years, we would have to conclude that the problem can be inherited.

If you have had the problem more than once, it would be helpful for you to gather all your pedigrees and do some detective work. By following the rules of recessive versus dominant inheritance, you can at least sort things out in a simple way. To determine whether it is a simple recessive or something more complex will take a great deal more pedigree information than most individuals have available to them.

Breeders and owners seem to have difficulty differentiating between three groups of problems that may affect a dog's limbs: (1) genetic or hereditary, (2) trauma secondary to true accidents and (3) changes secondary to aging.

When you repeatedly breed to a genetic problem, you increase its incidence and possibly worsen it. A genetic problem cannot correct itself except through the almost nonexistent chance of a mutation taking place. Thus, it is never wise to ignore a genetic problem.

Common sense should tell you when true accidents have occurred. An accident that results in trauma in the birth canal due to improper positioning of the pup will not necessarily recur when the bitch is bred again.

A sound-limbed puppy or adult that suffers an injury resulting in a damaged extremity may not be a candidate for the show ring, but this would have no effect on the dog's genetic makeup.

Dogs develop degenerative osteoarthritis with age, much as humans do. The degree of involvement may vary from one dog or line to the other.

Skipping or hopping is seen in Beagles without any evidence of slipped stifle or hip dysplasia. It has been suggested that the problem may lie with the fabellae, which are tiny sesamoid bones of the stifle joint. Two of these are located within the tendon of the gastrocnemius muscle, and the third is in the popliteus muscle. These little bones facilitate the motion of the stifle joint.

Osteochondritis Dissecans (OCD)

One case of OCD in Beagles has been reported. This disease involves the articular (joint) cartilage and underlying bone with inflammation and production of "joint mice," which are intra-articular loose bodies. Most often, the shoulder joint is affected in other breeds, although sometimes several joints can be involved. In the Beagle reported, multiple joints were affected, and the four-and-one-half-month puppy that was the subject of the report was euthanized.

Some cases heal with rest; others require surgical removal of loose joint bodies and the scraping of affected underlying bone.

Short Chest or Pigeon Breast

The Beagle with the "pigeon breast" condition presents a shortened and markedly curved sternum or breastbone. The number of ribs is normal. This condition is most easily discovered by the feel of the puppy when it is held with one hand under the chest. With the dog standing in profile, if you look carefully, it is evident as a "tuck up" that is closer to the front end of the Beagle than normal.

Not enough data are available yet to speculate on the mode of transmission. However, because pigeon breast has occurred in two generations, it is a genetic defect.

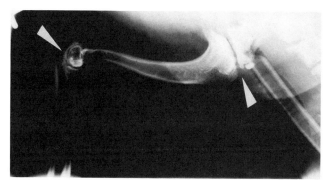

A radiograph of Banty's left shoulder and elbow showing degenerative joint disease of the shoulder and a misshapen elbow joint.

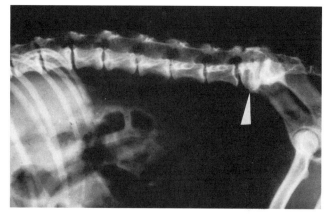

A radiograph of Banty's lumbar spine at age six, showing wedge-shaped deformed L-7 vertebra and decreased disc spaces between verebrae.

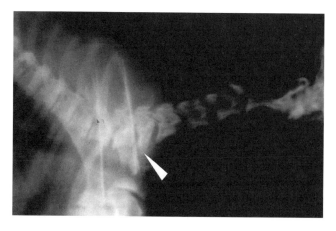

A radiograph of Banty's cervical spine with wedge-shaped C-6 vertebra and narrowed intervertebral disc spaces.

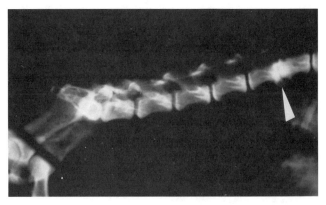

A radiograph of the lumbar spine in a nonaffected adult Beagle demonstrating the normal shape of vertebral bodies and intervertebral disc thickness. The marker points to the site of the intervertebral disc disease.

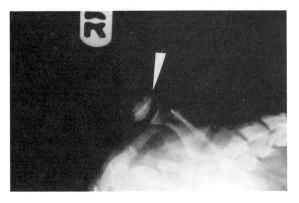

"Red"—A radiograph of the front extremity showing increased density of the upper end of the upper arm bone (humerus) at six weeks of age. The best time for x-ray diagnosis is at eight weeks.

"Red" at six weeks. The radiograph shows destruction of the elbow joint, including both the lower end of the humerus and the upper end of the ulna.

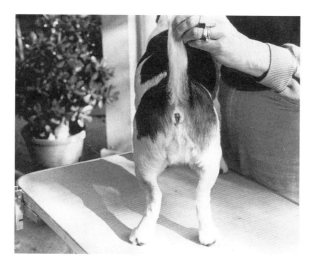

Boom Boom. Note the deformity of the hind legs.

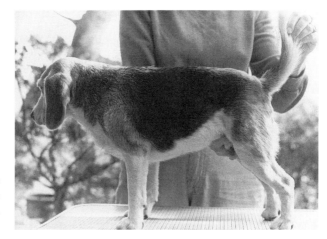

Banty, an adult male with a less severe form of chondrodystrophy.

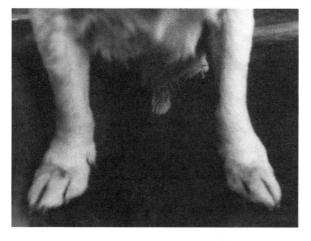

Banty, showing a typical deformity of the front legs.

Pigeon breast poses no known health problems for the dog but should be considered a defect as far as breeding is concerned.

Short Outer Toes on the Front Feet

This condition is not an uncommon occurrence. It usually appears in a very tight, small foot with very straight pasterns, with the outer toe foreshortened. Breeders have reported the rare occurrence of more than one toe on a foot being short, as well as additional toes and pads (supernumeraries) on the top of an otherwise normal-looking foot.

Once again, we do not have enough data as of the present to speculate on the mode of transmission, except to say that this condition seems to occur in certain lines.

Intervertebral Disc Disease

Intervertebral discs are little "cushions" between the vertebral bodies that function basically as shock absorbers and produce mobility of the spinal column. Aging results in degenerative changes that can vary in the rate of development and severity, causing chronic pressure on the spinal cord or nerve roots. Acute signs of intervertebral disc disease can be present if there is actual prolapse or rupture of disc material.

Degenerative disc disease appears to occur earlier and to progress more rapidly in the achondroplastic breeds. Because Beagles are considered achondroplastic, it is not unusual to observe the manifestation of the disease process as early as three to six years of age.

Symptoms: The dog generally exhibits a pain pattern: limited activity, depression (tail down) and even a loss of appetite (which is almost unimaginable!).

We have found in our kennel that most of an affected Beagle's symptoms will respond to crate rest and the administration of corticosteroids. However, a veterinarian should always be consulted. Rarely, when signs of nerve compression progress in spite of conservative measures, neurosurgical intervention is required. Although this type of intervention is expensive and requires careful follow-up care, the Beagle can have many years of active and happy life remaining.

Crooked Tails

Occasionally, a Beagle will have a tail with an obvious bend or angle in the line of the tail vertebrae, producing the appearance of a "kink" in the tail.

X-rays of such a tail show that two vertebrae are fused together, reducing the natural flexible curve. This condition occurs most commonly at the base and tip of the tail.

"Pigeon breast."

"Pigeon breast" is more apparent in this position.

Short outer toe.

A good, full brush obscures the small, bony deformity, which is most easily discovered by running your hand along the full course of the tail. When the fusion is at the base, the tail may appear to have a "gay carriage."

Some Beagle lines have produced several individuals with fused vertebrae at the base of the tail, but once again, the data are only suggestive of an inheritable condition.

Usually, this slight deformity is barely visible and certainly does not detract from the Beagle's working ability or its appearance in the conformation ring.

Bites

Occasional reports of bad bites crop up each year. Most of these occur in only one puppy in a litter. Rarely is an entire litter affected, although it has happened.

Overbites are more common than underbites, and each appears to be relatively line-specific. A wry bite—one side scissors and the other undershot and open—also occurs in Beagles.

OTHER PROBLEM AREAS

Chinese Beagle Syndrome

Your bitch has delivered normally. One of the puppies appears to have a different-looking head with a wide skull and wide-set eyes that are somewhat slanted. At three or four weeks, the puppy appears stiff when moving about. By ten to twelve weeks, there are signs of a short outer toe on some of the feet. When running, the puppy "bunny hops." The skin feels hard and stiff. In other respects, the puppy appears just like its siblings. By four to six months, the stiffness of the legs has increased until the pup walks on the center two toes, unable to flex its pasterns. The condition stabilizes by about one year of age. Unless there are associated congenital or genetic problems, your young dog will have a happy, normal life span.

What is this syndrome? We really don't know.

Occurrence: Since first reported in 1990, twenty-three (and probably four or five more) affected puppies have been documented in the United States and Canada. Similar Beagles appeared in Australia and England in the early 1970s. Efforts to obtain records of the Australian Beagles studied at a veterinary center there have proved fruitless. The two or three English Beagles described by Douglas Appleton were from the same family.

Nikki, an adult "Chinese Beagle." Note the broad skull and short outer toes. Affected animals will adopt the typical stance of standing on their toes with a lack of flexion in the metatarsal-tarsal joints.

Of the twenty-three reported since 1990, two Beagles have associated heart defects—one with multiple defects and the other with pulmonary stenosis (narrowing of the pulmonary valve). The Beagle with the heart defect also had grand mal seizures. Nine are dead. Seven of the nine were euthanized: four when the problem was first noted, two for pain and one for associated blindness. Diagnostic studies were performed on two of the dogs prior to euthanasia, and postmortem studies were carried out on brain and muscle tissue.

One affected Beagle died at fifteen years of age. The remaining fifteen are all alive and reportedly doing well.

Diagnosis: Because this syndrome has not been reported in the veterinary literature available to us, these affected Beagles have been an interesting puzzle for their owners and attending veterinarians.

X-rays of the dogs show only the shortened outer toe with otherwise normal bone and joint development. Electromyography (testing of the electrical potential of the muscles mediated through the nerves that supply them) on two Beagles showed a generalized abnormality suggestive of spinal cord, spinal nerve root and/or peripheral nerve disorder.

Gary Johnson, DVM, genetic researcher with the University of Missouri School of Veterinary Medicine, noted similarities in the appearance of affected Beagles and humans afflicted with pseudohypopara-thyroidism or Albright's hereditary osteodystrophy—a genetic disorder in which target cells in the kidney and bone are unable to respond to normal amounts of parathyroid hormone. The humans show defects in growth and skeletal development, are short in stature with short hand and foot bones, have short necks and display evidence of calcification under the skin. So far, testing of the Chinese Beagles, though planned, has not been performed.

Primary hypoparathyroidism has occured in the Miniature Schnauzer; however, it differs significantly from our Chinese Beagle Syndrome.

Another likely possibility, according to H.W. Leipold, DVM, Professor of Pathology, College of Veterinary Medicine, Kansas State University, is a familial neuronal abiotrophy—an inherited failure of the nerve cells of the central nervous system to develop properly. Sections of the brain, spinal cord, and skeletal muscle of two two-and-one-half-month-old affected puppies studied at the University of Saskatchewan Veterinary School in the early 1980s showed abnormalities in skeletal muscle, increased number of cells in the spinal cord, and many changes in the cellular structure of the brain. The pathologist's conclusion was that the muscle damage was most likely the result of defective nerve supply, and the brain changes were most suspicious of familial neuronal abiotrophy.

Genetics: Not enough pedigrees are available to provide a decisive analysis. It is clear, however, that certain families have more affected puppies than

Joey, a "Chinese Beagle" puppy. Note the oblique eye-set, the typical sitting position of those affected, the short outer toes and the developing stiffness of the foot joints.

other families. If breeders treat this as a simple recessive, then any dog or bitch producing an affected puppy is an automatic carrier. Remember that two carriers bred to each other will result in 25 percent affected, 50 percent carriers and 25 percent clear.

"Drunken" or Tumbling Puppies

One of the puppies in your litter is slow to get to its feet. When it finally does, it moves unsteadily, with a tendency to fall to the same side. Its head may be tilted, and sometimes a rapid horizontal flicking of the eyeballs is evident. As the puppy reaches ten to twelve weeks, circling, difficulty maintaining its balance and easy falling are obvious. Frankly, the puppy acts drunk! As it matures, symptoms stabilize and may even improve somewhat. There appears to be a range of afflictions. The mildly or moderately affected are able to adjust to pet homes. The severely afflicted must be euthanized. The puppies that do accommodate do better in homes with flat yard surfaces and not too many obstacles.

Diagnosis: Since 1991, thirteen such puppies have been reported. All demonstrate the same symptoms.

Diagnoses have included cerebellar hypoplasia (failure of the balance center of the brain to develop fully), middle-ear problems, congenital middle-ear problems and cerebellar abiotrophy (abnormal development of the brain cells in the balance and coordination center of the brain). The latter diagnosis was made from pathological sections of the brain from a euthanized puppy.

Management: A thorough examination by a qualified veterinarian is essential. Similar symptoms can occur in a hydrocephalic puppy. Findings on examination should differentiate between these conditions.

These puppies will simply require the usual care of any growing Beagle, but with care taken to protect them from falling from heights or tumbling into pits or trenches. Spaying or neutering is essential. With these precautions, these puppies can live out a normal, happy life span.

Genetics: The number of affected Beagles is not great enough to state that this condition is a genetic problem. However, the pedigrees are suggestive. The literature on cerebellar abiotrophies in other mammals list it as inherited. There is a bilateral vestibular (balance) dysfunction reported in Miniature Schnauzer puppies from birth resulting in ataxia (unsteadiness of gait), a bobbing or rotary movement of the head and deafness, thesyndrome said to be of recessive inheritance. So far, none of the Beagle puppies that have been reported to us have been deaf.

Tooth and Gum Disease

Beagles have a reputation for early development of tartar (brown stains), calculus (layers of tartar) and gum disease. Some conformation lines show a greater tendency toward this condition than others.

Occasionally, pitting and staining of the permanent teeth are visible. Though commonly known as "distemper teeth," this destruction of the tooth enamel can occur as a result of a high fever or use of certain antibiotics, such as tetracycline, in a puppy at the time of permanent tooth eruption.

We have seen this condition develop in young Beagles with *no* history of high fever or exposure to antibiotics. Breeders of Standard Poodles and Miniature Schnauzers have reported similar experiences.

At least in the affected Beagle population, the pattern of distribution strongly suggests an inherited tendency.

Good preventive dental hygiene begun early delays the onset of tooth and gum problems. Regular cleaning by your veterinarian will probably be required.

Bleeding Tendency

Von Willebrand's Disease (vWD), an inherited bleeding disorder, commonly occurs in a number of dog breeds. Though an occasional case of vWD in Beagles has been reported, the disease does not appear to be a serious threat at this time. However, any Beagle that demonstrates slow clotting time—any cut or overly-trimmed toenail that does not clot within two or three minutes—should be tested by a veterinarian.

For a more complete discussion of von Willebrand's Disease, see the "Dominance Inheritance" section in Chapter 15.

Umbilical Hernia

This condition, a protrusion through the opening in the abdominal wall at the site of the umbilical cord, is caused by a genetic predisposition for delayed closure of the abdominal ring.

Small umbilical hernias are common in Beagles and require no treatment. Surgical repair should be carried out if the defect is large enough to admit a fingertip through the ring.

Ch. Merry Song's Top Performance, thirteen-inch dog, and Ch. Merry Song's Star Performance, thirteen-inch bitch (Ch. Merry Song's High Performance ex Merry Song's Bit of Honey), shown winning one of five Best Brace in Show awards they have acquired. They are owned by Drs. Mara Baun and Nancy Bergstrom. *Melia*

chapter 17

Coat-Color Inheritance

Geneticists have postulated many coat-color genes, but we will deal mainly with the four colors of greatest interest to Beaglers: (1) tricolor, (2) lemon or red and white, (3) blue and (4) liver or chocolate. In the following explanation, we have leaned heavily on Clarence C. Little's *Inheritance of Coat Color in Dogs* (New York: Howell Book House, 1957).

The degree of expression of a gene may vary from animal to animal. This may be due to other genes modifying the effect of the genes in question. Difference in expression may also be due to other alleles (either of two genes that occupy the same locus). The case in which the effects of a gene are expressed in some animals and not in others is termed "incomplete penetrance." Also, there are many genes that have small, modifying effects on color or patterns, sometimes acting at different ages, that tend to obscure the effects of the major genes.

Although only two alleles can be present at a locus in one animal, multiple alleles often exist in the population as a whole. The locus involved in the coat color of the Beagle is an example of this. This chapter lists these loci and their various allelic possibilities. This information can be seen with other color patterns in Little's book.

Because of the complexity and the difficulty in determining the various fine shades of color, we have eliminated detailed information concerning inheritance of different degrees of redness, tanness and the various grades of spotting or intensity of coat colors.

GENES FOR COLOR BELIEVED PRESENT IN BEAGLES

Each individual will have two genes for each locus; the highest ranking member at any locus will be seen in the phenotype.

The genes Beagles are believed to carry are listed in order of relative dominance, top to bottom, at each locus. When only one gene is shown at a locus, it indicates that the Beagle is homozygous for that gene. By "relative dominance," we mean that certain genes, whether they are dominant or recessive, are more dominant than others at the same locus and therefore have a higher rank from top to bottom.

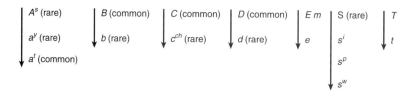

Locus A: Allows or restricts formation of dark (black or brown) pigment. A^s: Allows distribution of dark pigment over whole body (self or solid color) as in the Newfoundland; rare in Beagles.

a^y: Restricts dark pigment greatly and, in most complete expression, produces a clear sable or tan dog, as in the Basenji. This type of red, tan or sable is doubtful in Beagles; most clear yellows or tans are the *ee* type (described later).

a^t: Produces tan points (black and tan or liver and tan, for example) To the best of our knowledge, all Beagles are homozygous for *at*, no matter what their color—even lemon and white.

aw: This gene is not included under Beagles in Little's book, but since we have had a few dogs with this hair pattern, we have included it for your information. The "wild color" gene allows for a banded type of hair. In *at* type dogs, the banded hair is restricted to certain areas, usually along the neck in Beagles.

Locus B: Determines whether dark pigment formed at *A* will be black or brown (brown includes liver and chocolate). Tricolored Beagles are *Bb* or *BB*. Liver- or chocolate-colored Beagles are *bb*.

Locus C: Basic factor for color, as distinguished from albinism.
C: Rich pigmentation, resulting in dark tan or red areas and absolute black or liver areas.
c^{ch}: Reduces richness of pigmentation, but usually its effect is visible to the eye only on red, tan or yellow pigment areas, which become lighter in shade toward lemon, buff or cream.

Locus D: The dilution factor for dark pigment.
D: Causes black or brown to remain black or brown.
d: Dilutes black to so-called Maltese blue (actually, gray) and brown to silvery, as in the Weimaraner. The dog must be *dd* to be "blue"—that is, both parents contributed a gene for the color to appear.

Locus E: The extension factor for dark pigment.

E: Allows dark pigment (black, brown or their diluted forms if affected by *dd)* to extend throughout the areas where produced.

e: Prevents extension of dark pigment, leaving the animal clear red, tan or yellow in pigmented (non-white) areas. The dog must be *ee* to be lemon or red and white.

Locus *M*: The dominant merle (*m*) factor, as in Collies. This has not been observed in Beagles; therefore, they are presumed to be of the formula *mm* (non-merle).

Locus *S*: The spotting factor.

S: Causes pigmentation of the entire surface—no white, except possibly an isolated spot, as on the chest; this is rare in Beagles.

s^i: Irish spotting (white feet, legs and chest) and blaze (a pretty definite pattern, as in the Basenji).

s^p: Piebald spotting. Colored head and blanket, with the rest of the surface white; this is the usual distribution in Beagles. There is a whole range of spotting, which is described in Little's book.

s^w: Extreme white piebald spotting; dog is almost pure white, except for dark patches at the eye, ear or near the base of the tail. Because there is considerable variation in the amount of spotting, it is sometimes difficult to differentiate between the lower type except by breeding tests to check progeny.

Locus *T*: The ticking factor.

T: Allows ticks of the dog's dark pigment color to appear in white areas.

t: Absence of ticks in white areas.

These loci have been named after the traits they represent, and to simplify the notations, they have been abbreviated. Thus, for example, *D* stands for the dilution factor. If there are more than a few alleles, then another letter is added to help describe the trait, as in *at*, the allele that allows for tan points. The inheritance of pigmentation, including color and patterns, is generally complex. Also, as previously observed, many genes have small, modifying effects on color or patterns, sometimes acting at different ages. These tend to obscure the effects on color or patterns, and sometimes act at different ages. Their influence may alter the effects of the major genes.

In addition, genes that are dominant are written as capital letters, and those that are recessive are written in lowercase letters. In the Beagle, all the loci involving coat color exist but are never expressed in their dominant forms. For example, the gene *As* would produce a completely black Beagle, and none has ever been recorded, or at the *M* locus, which would produce a merle dog. The point of all this is that the Beagle does carry two genes at these loci, but the traits they represent are never seen.

With respect to the genes *A, B, D,* and *E,* one Beagle can carry the genes for all four of the coat colors under discussion. It should also be apparent that the term "dominant for tri" is a misnomer, since the gene for triness is actually recessive.

You can also see that blues are simply tricolors that are homozygous for the dilution factor. They will have the genes *atat dd E?*. The question mark means that the other gene at the locus can be either *E* or *e; s*, as the dominant form, will mask any *e* gene.

In the same vein, you can see that the lemon-and-white Beagle is a homozygous tri that is also homozygous for the recessive form of the *E* gene. This dog will have the genes *atat D? ee*. Again, the question mark represents the idea that the gene at this locus can be either *D* or *d*.

Have you ever seen a red, white and blue Beagle? Believe it or not, they do exist. This dog will have the genes *atat dd ee* and will generally look like a lemon-and-white Beagle, but tan points will be duller in color than normal.

The next question for the breeder interested in the color of his dogs is how carriers of these recessive genes can be detected. The answer is by test breeding. You can now refer to the "Progeny Testing" section in Chapter 15, "Genetics: How Can I Use What I Don't Understand?" to see how a test breeding is done and what the chances are for getting any one of the colors you want.

SAMPLE COLORS AND GENETIC PATTERN

a^ta^t *B? C? D? E? mm sP? tt:* tricolor (black blanket, tan points, no ticking)

a^ta^t *bb C?D? E? mm sP? tt:* tricolor (liver blanket, tan points, no ticking)

a^ta^t *B? C? dd E? mm sP? tt:* tricolor (blue blanket, dull yellow points)

a^ta^t *B? C? D? ee mm sP? tt:* red and white (white dog with varying degrees of tan or red patches). If the genotype at the C locus was *Cch*, the dog would have rich pigment but could throw pups in which the tan is reduced to buff.

a^ta^t *B? chch ee mm sP?:* lemon and white (white dog with lemon or buff patches)

a^ta^t *B?C? dd ee mm sP?:* red, white and blue (very patriotic—would look like a lemon-and-white dog with dull, buff points, light nose and eye pigment)

Where question marks appear, the other gene of the pair for the locus may be either dominant or recessive—only test breeding will give you the answer.

As an example, suppose that you have a liver (chocolate) maiden bitch that you want to breed to a tricolor male that has produced lemon-and-white puppies, and you want to know what your chances will be of getting tricolor puppies.

We know a little about your bitch's genotype because of her unusual color. It is *atat bb C? D? E? mm sP: tt*. We are not concerned with the *D, M, S* or *T* loci at this time, so we can disregard them for now.

We also know that the bitch is homozygous for *at* (it is tricolor) and *b* (its color is liver). The possible combinations for the bitch during segregation follow:

a^{t}bCE   a^{t}bCe

^{t}bcE   a^{t}bce

Because of the male's color and the puppies he has produced, we also know something about his genotype. It is *a^{t}a^t B? C? D? Ee mm sP? tt*. We know that the dog is homozygous for *a^t* (it is tricolored) and that he has produced lemon-and-white puppies. The possible combinations for the dog during segregation follow:

a^{t}BCE   a^{t}BCe

a^{t}BcE   a^{t}Bce

a^{t}bCE   a^{t}bCe

a^{t}bcE   a^{t}bce

Using Punnett's Square, a breeder could determine possible colors in a forthcoming litter:

		BITCH			
		a¹bCE	a¹bCe	a¹bcE	a¹bce
	a¹BCE	a¹a¹BbCCEE tricolor	a¹a¹CCEe tricolor	a¹a¹BbCcEE tricolor	a¹a¹BbCcEe tricolor
	a¹BCe	a¹a¹BbCCEe tricolor	a¹a¹BbCCee red & white	a¹a¹BbCcEe tricolor	a¹a¹BbCcee red & white
	a¹BcE	a¹a¹bCcEE tricolor	a¹a¹BbCcEe tricolor	a¹a¹BBCcEE tricolor buff points	aa¹BbccEe tricolor buff points
D O G	a¹Bce	a¹a¹BbCcEe tricolor	a¹a¹BbCcee red & white	a¹a¹BbccEe tricolor buff points	a¹a¹Bbccee lemon & white
	a¹bCE	a¹a¹bbccee liver	a¹a¹bbCCEe liver	a¹a¹bbCcEE liver	a¹a¹bbCcEe liver
	a¹bCe	a¹a¹bbCCEe liver	a¹a¹bbCCee red & white w/bb color?	a¹a¹bbCcEe liver	a¹a¹bbCcee red & white
	a¹bcE	a¹a¹bbCcEE liver	a¹a¹CcEe liver	a¹a¹bbccEE liver buff points	a¹a¹bbccEe liver buff points
	a¹bce	a¹a¹bbCcEe liver	a¹a¹bbCcee red & white w/bb color?	a¹a¹bbccEe liver buff points	a¹a¹bbccee lemon & white buff points bb masked?

If the male carries the gene for the liver and the female carries the gene for the lemon and white, your statistical possibilities would be 12 tri: 12 liver: 6 red and white: 2 lemon and white. Your chances of getting a tri are 12 out of 32, or 37.5 percent. Remember the numbers for progeny testing: If out of six puppies, none are red and white, there is a 95 percent chance that the bitch does not carry that gene. If there are no liver puppies, there is a 95 percent chance that the dog does not carry that gene.

Normally, with three genes, there would be sixty-four possible combinations, so you can see how knowing more information about these dogs would simplify these probabilities. You could also have eliminated the C gene to simplify it further.

In brief, the tricolor coat, although inherited as a recessive, is dominant (less recessive) over the lemon or red and white gene, which is also inherited recessively.

The blue color is not a color at all, but a dilution of one of the other colors. We usually see a tri Beagle with the dilution factor. This gives the black saddle a bluish cast and the tan points a correspondingly duller color. However, a lemon and white or liver and white can also show a dilute effect.

As far as the importance of the colors themselves, please refer to the Beagle Standard. However, there are some interesting points that might be considered. According to one author, there is evidence that Collies homozygous for the dilution factor dd have lower intelligence and are less resistant to infections. It should be noted that the dilution effect in Collies and Beagles is not the same as merling (also known as dappling). The merle pattern consists of an irregular patchwork of two contrasting colors, such as black with blue-gray. The blue Beagles we have been acquainted with have thinner coats than our Standard calls for and seem to be more susceptible to skin problems.

On the other hand, lemon-and-white dogs would be expected to be more resistant to the ill effects of a hot, sunny day than darker-coated dogs.

Punnett's Square is a sure and graphical way to illustrate how gene pairs might be inherited. However, it becomes unwieldy very quickly when you do three-gene pairs that have sixty-four possible combinations.

This brings up the main problem in breeding dogs. With an average of four to five puppies per litter, it is not possible for more than half the possible nine combinations in a two-gene pair characteristic to occur. It would probably take several litters before a desired recessive would turn up. This might even be the case for a characteristic inherited through a one-gene pair. Given these poor odds, it should become obvious why we have so much difficulty getting or keeping a quality such as good movement, which probably has many genes involved in its creation.

To complete your frustration, there is the case of chromosomal inheritance. The dog has thirty-nine chromosome pairs; humans have only twenty-three. During reduction division, the chromosome pairs separate, one of each pair going into one or the other side of the nucleus. The nucleus then divides,

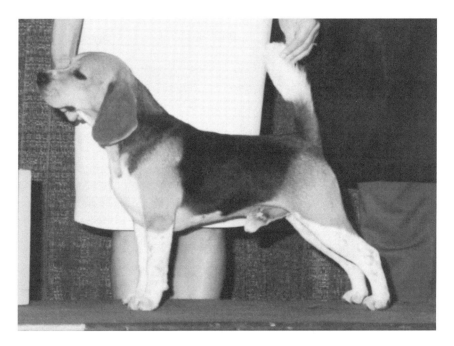

Ch. Dreams of Cadillac Style, thirteen-inch dog (Ch. Lanbur Coupe de Ville ex Merry
Music Chantilly Lace), multiple Group winner, owned by Teresa Malinski and Ed
Seyle. *Bonnie Gray*

Ch. Meadowland's Blaze of Glory, fifteen-inch bitch (Ch. Wilkat's Teddy Caboose
ex Ch. Lee's Wild Peaches N' Cream). Best of Opposite Sex to Best of Breed, NBC
Specialties, 1995 and 1996, owned by Bruce and Shirley Irwin. *Tom di Giacomo*

leaving each half with thirty-nine chromosomes, one of each kind. The key to this is that, as far as we know, it is pure chance how the chromosomes line up before cell division, and consequently the proportion of contribution from each grandparent will vary.

A method to illustrate this process for you is suggested by Anne Paramoure in *Breeding and Genetics of the Dog* (Middleburg, VA, Denlinger, 1959).

Take two sets of poker chips or paper—for example, red and white poker chips. Number each set 1 through 39. Mix them together in a bowl and then draw them out one at a time. Arrange them into two piles, 1 through 39.

When you have finished, you will have two piles numbering thirty-nine each. But they will not be all the same color in either pile. (Well, they could, but it is extremely unlikely.)

You can let red represent the sire and white the dam, and the two piles will represent the two halves of the germ cell in reduction division.

This can be enlarged by setting up another group with blue and yellow chips representing your bitch (be sure to discard one pile, which would represent the polar body that is discarded in reduction division of the female). Now add the male chromosomes, giving you seventy-eight chromosomes, or thirty-nine pairs.

Now set up two equal piles. Each pile represents just one of the possible chromosome combinations your puppies might inherit. How many chips represent each of the grandparents? If you keep selecting different combinations, you will see that it is possible that one of the grandparents might not be represented at all.

Now put all the chips back and do it again. No matter what you got the first time, it will be different the second time. Even if the colors were the same, you would find that the chromosome numbers are different.

Again, the exception to this is when a mutation occurs—let's hope you all find the equivalent of the Morgan horse in your kennel!

chapter 18

Life Cycle of a Dog Fancier

Dog fanciers don't just happen—they don't just burst forth full-grown like Athena from Zeus's forehead. Either they are born to the fancy or acquire the passion in later years. Growing up with parents who spend weekends showing or running their dogs can have a powerful impact on children. Some will love it and continue to be involved throughout their adult lives. Others resent the dog fancy's impact on their childhoods and are only too glad to be free of it. For those who stumble into organized dog activities later in life, the process is similar to falling in love. The initial attraction either fizzles out, since the average life of a dog exhibitor is about five years, or develops into a passionate, lifetime commitment.

Humans, like dogs, are highly territorial and competitive animals. Feelings can run high in a sport where there is only one Best of Breed. Even the most civilized people can be reduced to being sore losers.

When dog activities are the only leisure interest, even more of one's self becomes focused on the outcome of shows. "Love me, love my dog" is the rule of the day. Involvement in at least one or two unrelated interests helps to maintain a sense of equilibrium.

If both spouses in a family are not comfortable with dog-related activities, then trouble may lie ahead. Both need not be equally involved, but the "passive" partner needs to support the spouse's interest. Often, both spouses are required to handle the associated workload.

Competition exerts tremendous pressure on friendships within the sport. Everyone loves a loser. The consistent winner inspires at least feelings of ambivalence. Joint breeding programs and co-ownerships can help. However, delicate nurturing of special friendships will require tact and empathy.

Let's face it. Dog shows are not like a golf game.

IN THE BEGINNING

Most of us start with a pet dog. Some go to a local dog show to look at various breeds prior to purchasing a family pet. That first contact with dog activities may be enough to snap the trap. If people are having fun, if the dogs are good-looking and happy and if the exhibitor/breeder approached for information is helpful and persuasive, then a decision just may be made to invest in a good show prospect.

Once the investment is made and the new puppy is home, training should begin. Contact with the original breeder, other Beaglers and attendance at puppy matches fuel the excitement. If the puppy is good enough, and you work hard to learn good handling techniques, wins will come at all-breed shows. Usually, it takes longer for novice exhibitors to take their dog to its championship. However, the fun of handling your own dog makes the additional time and effort worth it.

Dog show days become social occasions where people discuss dogs endlessly. Indeed, the mark of a "real Beagle person" is an ability to discuss every detail of the hound's ancestry, appearance, personality, digestive tract functions and wins and losses *ad nauseam*. This typical form of communcation is readily recognizable. Before long, you may find yourself going this route; you should enjoy the trip.

Along the way, you may try some Obedience work with your Beagle and most likely will join either a local all-breed club or a Beagle Specialty Club if there is one nearby.

Your Beagle has acquired its championship. The next major decision must now be made. If your Beagle is a bitch, should you breed her and begin again with a new puppy? Should you campaign your Beagle as a champion in competition with other champion Beagles with an eye toward competition beyond the breed level? Obviously, the decision about showing a champion male is not affected by breeding.

THE CAMPAIGN

"Specialing" a dog is the term given to showing a champion. If you elect to Special your Beagle, you must realize that this is a totally different ball game from showing in the regular classes. Wins at Variety level are exciting, but competition at Hound Group or Best in Show levels constitutes the "big high." The excitement can truly become addictive as you work for the top prizes. Competition at these levels requires several essentials: a good Beagle, a good handler and the time and money to see the campaign through successfully.

Certainly not all Beagles that are campaigned successfully are exceptional representatives of the breed, but they all have one thing in common: they are "show dogs." These are dogs that love to please, love to show and will give their all in the ring. They have a "look at me" attitude that often carries them to great achievements.

Sarabanda's Oberon, fifteen-inch dog (Ch. Dreams of Son of a Sailor ex Ch. Omar Dreams of a Dozen Roses), at three months. A winner of Best Puppy in Group at nine months in Argentina, he was bred by Ruby Perdomo, Columbia, S.A.

Campaigning a Special does not mean showing at an occasional show. It means exhibiting at most of the shows in your geographical area and frequently well beyond it, depending on the judging slates. If you handle your own dog, it requires personal travel almost every weekend of the year, and with the explosion of dog shows, frequently during the work week. Early mornings, long drives, difficult and wearing airline connections, time lost from home and long hours of grooming and caring for your Beagle on the campaign trail are all part of the package. Even if you hire a professional handler, you may have to transport the dog to and from the handler. And, of course, even with a professional handler, you will want to attend at least some shows as well.

Our experience has taught us that the Beagles that do not return home frequently between shows for contact with their normal routine and surroundings do not enjoy the shows after a time as much as those that do get time out for a little home time. They also need the rest and relaxation, much as humans do. The demands on owner, handler and dog are very stressful. During intensive campaigning, physiological changes can result in reduced sperm counts in dogs and delayed seasons in bitches.

Along with direct involvement in shows, time is also needed for peripheral dog activities. Remember that most owners of successful show dogs belong to their local all-breed kennel club and frequently to their national breed club. Making a contribution of time and work is an important part of the dog-show scene. Club meetings, days of preparation for the all-breed show and special projects are demanding but rewarding. As a working club member, you have opportunities to meet exhibitors and breeders of other breeds, American Kennel Club personnel and, last but not least, judges! All have much to teach.

Time is a precious and finite commodity. How you choose to spend it is a highly personal decision. When spent on dog activities, less time is available for families, children and other interests.

THE HANDLER

If you are not handling your Beagle yourself, you will require the services of a professional dog handler. Selecting the proper person for your needs requires some research. Of first concern will be the quality of care that will be given your Beagle. Cleanliness, good health and proper grooming make for proper presentation. Also, will your Beagle be happy and safe? Communication between owner and handler must be clear and open. Competition is stressful. The job demands someone who can lose as well as win gracefully, is respected by his or her peers and will preferably give you "first call" in the Hound Group.

A special rapport develops between handler and dog in a successful team. Also, the client/handler relationship can develop into a special friendship, one more reward in the dog game—potentially one of the richest.

MONEY

Campaigning your Beagle is a costly business. When making the decision, consider that entries at roughly sixty shows a year will cost about $1,200, and that handling fees and travel expenses can run into the several thousands: handling fees normally begin at $60 per show with "bonuses" for Group wins or placements. Charges for boarding and a share of travel expenses drive your outlay still higher. Photographs of your Beagle's wins run about $26 per show.

Don't forget the advertising in magazines and newspapers serving the dog fancy. Advertising has become an integral part of campaigning, whether you like it or not, since exposure on a monthly or more often basis improves your dog's chances of recognition in the show ring. Ads range from $175 to $350 per page.

To summarize, campaigning a Special can, at a conservative estimate, cost an owner about $1,500 per month. In many cases, it can amount to considerably more.

Obviously, campaigning is not for everyone.

THE NEXT GENERATION

Decisions about breeding, raising litters, selling and placing puppies and servicing either one's own or visiting bitches are tasks that come with this stage in the breeder's development. It truly requires two in a household in most instances to make a success of the dog fancy.

Requests for stud service are the natural consequence of a successful campaign and one of the reasons for it. Frankness about your stud's virtues, faults and genetic makeup are essential when dealing with owners of outside bitches.

Extensive correspondence, time-consuming phone calls, trips to airports, struggles with frightened bitches and sometimes difficult owners are standard. It may seem as though bitches are receptive only on Christmas day or during family holidays. Weekends and evenings are frequently interrupted by enthusiastic owners, complete with children and assorted relatives, along with their bitches in season.

Once we had a memorable occasion in dealing with the owner of a bitch, an elderly grandmother who spoke only Russian, and the owner's eight-year-old daughter who played the piano in the living room for the duration of the breeding. Her parting shot was a request for a quarter along with an invitation to the male half of our family to marry her. Fortunately, laughter eases difficult times.

Each litter sired by your stud becomes part of your extended dog family. What happens to them in part happens to you, too.

Delivering and raising a litter can be one of the joys of life with Beagles. Newborns are a marvel with their instinct for survival. Maternal behavior is astonishing to observe. Nothing is more fetching than six-week-old Beagle puppies. Born clowns, they tumble, cuddle, roughhouse and are always appealing. A good breeding produces promising puppies. What a thrill it is to watch a good puppy grow into an excellent adult!

But things do not always go well. Missed breedings, difficult deliveries, Caesarean sections in the middle of the night under less than ideal conditions and weak and failing puppies confront us all. As if that were not enough, there are always some puppies that are lost either in delivery or during the neonatal period, the uncovering of genetic defects theretofore undiscovered and the worry about infectious diseases. Sleepless nights spent feeding weak puppies, cleaning up after mother and offspring and visiting the veterinarian all take their toll. And finally, there is the emotional trauma when loved puppies leave for new homes.

Visits from prospective puppy owners bring unusual opportunities to observe family interaction. You've probably met them: the nice people who don't want to touch the dogs, the delightful young couple whose nine-year-old attempts to strangle his little friend behind the central kitchen counter while his five-year-old sibling sneakily knocks over the little puppies, and the family that must have a puppy the day before yesterday—and when arrangements are finalized to have the puppy available in two weeks, has a change of heart.

Most original homes are neither designed for dog breeders nor situated in appropriate neighborhoods. Inevitably, the search for country property begins with plans for a "real kennel." As a result of the burgeoning dog population and worry about potential complaints from neighbors, a major move is in order. Sometimes this involves becoming experts in septic systems, private water sources and roadbuilding, as well as dealing with the threat of mud slides, forest fires and other natural calamities.

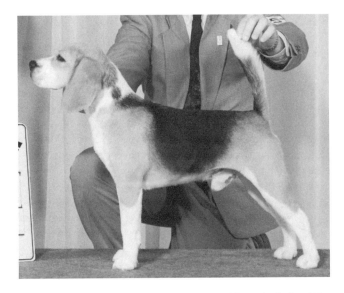

Am. & Can. Ch. Fircone Country Cousin, fifteen-inch dog (Ch. Lanbur Coupe de Ville ex Ch. Knolland Rose Bouquet), a multiple BIS and Group winner and Best of Breed, NBC Specialty, 1994, owned by Bill and Sue Gear. *Alex Smith*

Ch. Greenwood's Grady Tate, fifteen-inch dog (Ch. Greenwood's Ball Park Frank ex Ch. Greenwood's Dress Batik), a multiple BIS, Group and Specialty winner, owned by Bruce Tague, Mark Lister and John and Greta Haag.

Am., Aus. & Can. Ch.
Starbuck Hot an' Spicy, fif-
teen-inch bitch (Am. &
Aus. Ch. Torbay Too Hot
To Handle ex Ch. Merry
Song's Sugar and Spice), a
champion and a producer
of champions in three coun-
tries, owned by David and
Lesley Hiltz. *Booth*

Hard Times

Your time will come! In any breeding program, lean times are inevitable.
Breedings that look marvelous on paper sometimes produce disappointing
puppies. The appearance of previously unidentified genetic defects, breaks
in your vaccination program, loss of litters and missed breedings will test the
resolve of the most tenacious breeders. Outcrosses made to increase vigor and
fertility often bring new problems as well.

Fortunately, there is an ever-increasing reservoir of information
related to many of the problems encountered by the conscientious breeder.
Consultation with knowledgeable professionals and other breeders offers new
approaches. Don't be shy about asking for help. There will be others who
will readily ask for yours.

The Golden Years, or Life Is Not Over

You are now twenty or thirty years into your life as a breeder. Wiser, less
positive about many of the aspects of Beagling than you once were, you begin to cut back a little.

It is said that old age is a time of losses. This is true for an aging breeder
as well. Your life apart from dogs presents new tasks and challenges. Also,
by this time, a collection of aging Beagles requires special time and attention.
You attend fewer shows, breed an occasional litter, and wonder what life
would be without the dogs.

You may find satisfaction pursuing a career in judging. For those who
enjoy organization, more time can be devoted to their local all-breed club.
Volunteer service at the local Society for the Prevention of Cruelty to Animals or breed rescue is always needed. Who, after all, is better qualified than
an experienced breeder or dog lover to improve the lot of less fortunate
canines?

Or, you can always write a book!

© Ann Mackenzie. '88

chapter 19

Outstanding Producers—A Pedigree Study

Unfortunately, excellent conformation Beagles don't always reproduce their quality. And sometimes less-than-great show Beagles can prove wonderful producers.

Styles in Beagles seem to change cyclically as a top-winning male, one that varies in type from a previous top-winner, is used extensively at stud. Less obvious, but perhaps even more important, is the impact of particular Beagle dams.

The number of champions produced by a given Beagle *may* be a measure of its genetic potency but most definitely is related to the number of breedings and puppies resulting from these breedings. The sires and dams presented in this chapter, in alphabetical order, are those we feel have had the greatest impact on our breed in the 1990s. Ability to set a certain style or type was our primary consideration, not the number of get. Obviously, these Beagles will continue to produce more champion get in time.

It is noteworthy how often certain ancestors appear in many of the pedigrees of these Beagles.

Though not included in this chapter, the great Beagles of the past have left an indelible stamp on the pedigrees of today. For this, we treasure them.

Ch. Alamo's Crown Prince, fifteen-inch sire of fifteen champions. Owned by Phil and Elaine Baffert. *Missy Yuhl*

                Ch. Wandering Wind

          Ch. Jana Exodus

                Ch. Bowmanor's Prima Donna

Sire: Ch. Jana Yankee Doodle Dandy

                Ch. Jana Zipper

          Ch. Jana Golden Pixie

                Ch. Jana Golden Poppy O'Swanlake

                Ch. Teloca Patches Littl' Dickens

          Ch. Sure-Luv's Fran Ray's Bandit

                Ch. Sure-Luv's Heather Mist

Dam: Ch. Lanbur Punkin of Alamo

                Ch. Teloca Patches Littl' Dickens

          Ch. Lanbur Love Notes

                Ch. Lanbur Bonus Baby

Ch. Bayou Oaks Cappuccino, fifteen-inch Multiple BIS and Group Winner; fifteen-inch BOV NBC Specialty, 1993. Sire of eighteen champions. Owned by Alyce and Richard Gilmore. *Alverson*

Ch. Keith's Wilkeep Nicodemus

Ch. Starbuck's Full Count

Ch. Wilkeep Love Notes

Sire: Ch. Barmere's Mario Andretti

Ch. Linven's Super Star

Ch. Knolland Country Gal

Ch. Knolland Kortney

Ch. Keith's Wilkeep Nicodemus

Ch. Wilkeep's Bayou Classic

Ch. Wilkeep's Cover Girl

Dam: Ch. Bayou Oaks Violetta

Ch. Whisper's Inflation Fighter

Ch. Bayou Belladonna

Woodland Trails Dazzle Doll

Ch. Barmere's Mario Andretti, fifteen-inch sire of many champions, including two BIS winners. Owned by Barbara Cosgrove.

                         Ch. Hickorynuts Hangman

                Ch. Starbuck's Full Count

                         Ch. Starbuck's Meadow Song

Sire: Ch. Keith's Wilkeep Nicodemus

                         Ch. Bonus Jack of Starcrest

                Ch. Wilkeep Love Notes

                         Ch. Wilkeep Hello Dolly

                         Ch. Rockaplenty Wild Oats

                Ch. Linven's Super Star

                         Ch. Birchwood Liven Betsy Ross

Dam: Ch. Knolland Country Gal

                         Knolland Kernel

                Ch. Knolland Kortney

                         Johjean Jorgia

Ch. Beowulf's Mass in C Minor, thirteen-inch sire of twenty-five champions. Owned by Terri Giannetti and Ted Swedalla.

Ch. Page Mill On The Road Again

Ch. D'Capri's Uncle Remus

Tarr Hill Love Me Tender

Sire: Ch. White Acres Designer Label

Ch. Whisper's Inflation Fighter

Ch. White Acres Libby On The Label

White Acres Simplicity

Ch. Chrisette's Macho Man

Ch.. Bridal Vale Beowulf Moody Blue

Bridal Vale Kristina TDX

Dam: Ch. Beowulf Days of Wine and Roses

Ch. Whisper's Double Tough

Ch. Chrisette's Beowulf Kashmir

Ch. Shadyhollow Wind Storm

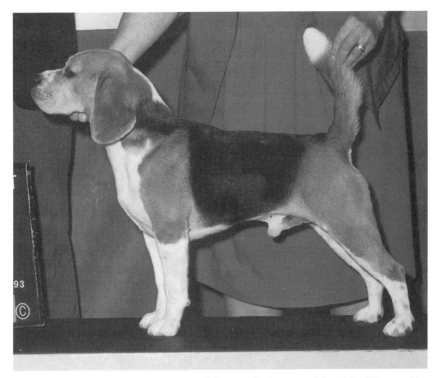

Ch. Daf-I-Dale's WillY 'R Wonty, CD, fifteen-inch Group and Specialty Winner. Sire of thirteen champions. Owned by Georgia and Vern Myers. *Steve Ross*

                  Ch. Hickorynuts Hangman

        Am., Can. Ch. Meadowcrest's Grand Slam

                  Am., Can. Ch. Starbuck's Meadow Song

Sire: Ch. Craigwood's Shyster

                  Ch. Swan Lakes Spirit of Craigwood

        Ch. Craigwood's Savvy

                  Ch. Craigwood's Shannon

                  Ch. Pickadilly Petticoat Chaser

        Ch. Pickadilly Westward Ho

                  Ch. Pickadilly Petticoat Legacy

Dam: Ch. Daf-I-Dale's Dusty Doll

                  Ch. Daf-I-Dale's Pardon My Dust

        Ch. Daf-I-Dale's Dust Devil, CD

                  Ch. Windy Ana of Daffodil Valley, UDT

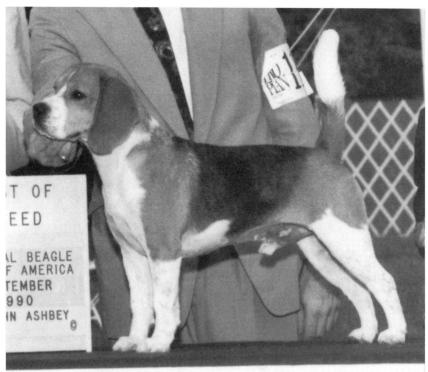

Ch. Lanbur the Company Car, fifteen-inch sire of over twenty-five champions. Group winner and 1990 NBC Specialty Best of Breed. Owned by Eddie Dzuik, Wade Burns and Jon Woodring. *Ashbey*

                       Ch. Teloca Patches On Target, CD

               Ch. Teloca Patches Littl' Dickens

                       Ch. Teloca Upstage Banned 'N Boston

Sire: Ch. Sure-Luv's Fran Ray Bandit

                       Ch. Navan's Triple Trouble Rick

               Ch. Sure-Luv's Heather Mist

                       Pixshire's Dark Victress

                       Ch. Hickorynut Hangman

               Ch. Craigwood Murphy

                       Ch. Craigwood Lucille

Dam: Ch. Stonebridge Lanbur Lady Luck

                       Ch. Pixshire's Trouble With Father

               Ch. Summerhill Cheez Cake

                       Ch. Summerhill Sara Lee

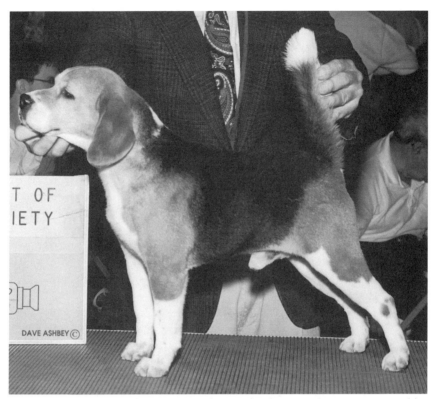

Ch. Lanbur Coupe De Ville, thirteen-inch sire of eighty-two champions. Owned by Jon Woodring and Wade Burns.

Ch. Teloca Patches Littl' Dickens

Ch. Sure-Luv's Fran Ray's Bandit

Ch. Sure-Luv's Heather Mist

Sire: Ch. Lanbur The Company Car

Ch. Craigwood's Murphy

Ch. Stonebridge Lanbur Lady Luck

Ch. Summerhill Cheez Cake

Ch. Meadow Crest Grand Slam

Ch. Craigwood's Shyster

Ch.. Craigwood Savvy

Dam: Ch. Altar's Lanbur Lacey J

Ch. Brantwood's Notorious

Ch. Pin Oaks Harper's Bazaar

Pin Oaks Sergeant Pepper

Ch. Merry Song's High Performance, fifteen-inch sire of at least sixteen champions. Group, BIS, and Specialty winner. Owned by Mara Baun and Nancy Bergstrom. *L. Sosa*

Ch. Wandering Wind

Ch. The Whim's Buckeye

The Whim's Firecracker

Sire: Ch. Starbuck's Hang 'Em High

Ch. Elsy's Jack Frost

Ch. Elsy's Shooting Star

Ch. Colegren Elsy's Lucky Star

Ch. Starbuck's Hang 'Em High

Ch. Merry Song's High and Mighty

Ch. Merry Song's Nutcracker

Dam: Ch. Merry Song's Ms Sunshine

Ch. Starbuck's Hang 'Em High

Ch. Merry Song's Uppity Ms

Ch. Sun Valley's Honey Bear

Ch. Page Mill On the Road Again, fifteen-inch Mult-Group and Specialty winner. Sire of many champions including two NBC Specialty BOBs. Owned by Carroll Diaz. *Mike Lidster*

                         Ch. Page Mill Stagehand

                Ch. Fulmont's Pub Crawler

                         Ch. Fulmont's Megan

Sire: Ch. Fulmont's Flashcube

                         Ch. Page Mill Trademark

                Ch. Fulmont's Fable

                         Ch. Fulmont's Megan

                         Ch. Jet's Gremlin of Starcrest

                Ch. Jana Nassau of Page Mill

                         Jana Ellie Belle

Dam: Ch. Page Mill Winnie The Pooh

                         Ch. White Acres No Fooling

                Page Mill Dawn of Starcrest

                         Ch. Page Mill Banter

Ch. Shaw's Mikey Likes It, fifteen-inch sire of thirty-two champions. Group winner; NBC Sire of the Year, 1990. Owned by John and Peggy Shaw. *Meyer*

Ch. The Whim's Buckeye

Ch. Starbuck's Hang 'Em High

Ch. Elsy's Shooting Star

Sire: Ch. Kamelot Shaw's Kome Lately

Plain and Fancy's Duke Gemini

Kamelot's Cactus Flower

Ch. Plain and Fancy's Clover

Ch. Busch's Flash Back of Eljon

Ch. Shaw's Watch Out For Hermie

Ch. Shaw's Spinning Wheel

Dam: Ch. Shaw's Ado Annie

Ch. Shaw's Watch Out For Hermie

Ch. Shaw's Ch.arm Bracelet

Ch. Shaw's I've Got Charm

Ch. Shaw's Spirit of the Chase, fifteen-inch sire of twenty champions. Group winner and NBC Award of Merit 1996. Owned by John and Peggy Shaw. *Booth*

                    Ch. Starbuck's Hang 'Em High

          Ch. Kamelot and Shaw's Kome Lately

                Kamelot's Kactus Flower

Sire: Ch. Shaw's Mikey Likes It

                Ch. Shaw's Watch Out For Hermie

          Ch. Shaw's Ado Annie

                Ch. Shaw's Charm Bracelet

                Ch. Craigwood's Wise Decision

          Ch. Stonebridge Winning Way

                Ch. Stonebridge Totally Awesome

Dam: Ch. Echo Run Kindred Spirit

                Timberlost's Trapper John

          Ch. Echo Run Shalamar

                Ch. Echo Run Heartbreaker CD

Ch. Sureluv's Chasin Rainbows, fifteen-inch Multiple BIS and Group winner. Sire of sixteen champions. Owned by Teresa Malinski. *Ashbey*

Ch. Teloca Patches On Target CD

Ch. Teloca Patches Littl' Dickens

Ch. Teloca Upstage Banned 'N Boston

Sire: Ch. Lanbur Roshan Hi Fidelity

Ch. Swan Lake's Spirit of Craigwood

Ch. Craigwood's Lucille

Craigwood's Baby Ruth

Ch. King's Creek Triple Threat

Ch. Navan's Triple Trouble Rick

Ch. Navan's Penny A Go Go CD

Dam: Ch. SureLuv's Heather Mist

Ch. Pixshire's Perfect Gentleman

Ch. Pixshire's Dark Victress

Ch. Pixshire's Whirling Dervish

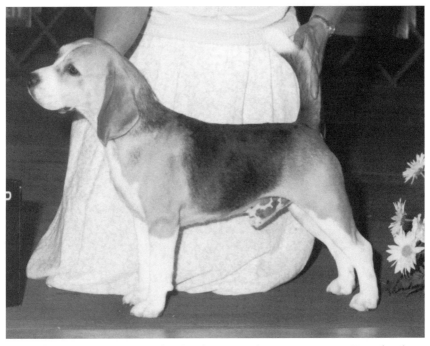

Ch. Swan Lake Fulmont's Fail Safe, thirteen-inch Group winner. Sire of at least fifteen champions. Owned by Dr. and Mrs. William Fulkerson. *Graham*

```
                    Ch. Fulmont's Pub Crawler
             Ch. Fulmont's Flash Cube
                    Ch. Fulmont's Fable
Sire: Ch. Page Mill On The Road Again
                    Ch. Jana Nassau of Page Mill
             Ch. Page Mill Winnie The Pooh
                    Ch. Page Mill Dawn of Starcrest
                    Ch. Swan Lake's Spirit of Craigwood
             Ch. Swan Lake Luke of Craigwood
                    Ch. Craigwood's Shannon
Dam: Ch. Swan Lake Fulmont's Fool Proof
                    Ch. Pixshire's The Entertainer
             Ch. Tarr Hill Classical Jazz
                    Ch. Tarr Hill's Triple Tina
```

Ch. Whiskey Creek's Jokeman, CD, fifteen-inch sire of fifteen champions. Owned by Michelle Sager and Tony Castellano.

                    Ch. Teloca Patches Littl' Dickens

            Ch. Meadow Crest's Fireside Chap

                    Ch. Starbuck's Meadow Song

Sire: Ch. Meadow Crest's Beau of Temateki

                    Kickapoo's Onyx Ed

            Ch. Sergeant Pepper's Sweet N' Low

                    Twiggly Wiggly

                    Ch. Hickorynuts Hangman

            Ch. Meadow Crest's Grand Slam

                    Ch. Starbuck's Meadow Song

Dam: Whiskey Creek's Pretender

                    Burrhus Frederick

            Ch. Felty Andrea of Frantz

                    Dalindale's Miss Min-De

Ch. White Acres Designer Label, fifteen-inch sire of over twenty champions. Owned by White Acre Kennels, Reg.

```
                          Ch. Fulmont's Flash Cube
               Ch. Page Mill On The Road Again
                          Ch. Page Mill Winnie The Pooh
Sire: Ch. D'Capri's Uncle Remus
                          Ch. Tarr Hill Rollikin' Romeo
               Tarr Hill Love Me Tender
                          Tarr Hill Samantha
                          Ch. Whisper's Call Me Mister
               Ch. Whisper's Inflation Fighter
                          Ch. Suntree's Pucker Pellet
Dam: Ch. White Acres Libby  On The Label
                          Ch. Validay Merry Monarch
               White Acres Simplicity
                          Ch. Whisper's Wisp O' Wind
```

Ch. Alamo's Hot To Trot of Lanbur, thirteen-inch dam of sixteen champions. Owned by Phil and Elaine Baffert. *Callea*

               Ch. Wandering Wind

         Ch. Jana Exodus

               Ch. Bowmanor's Prima Donna

Sire: Ch. Jana Yankee Doodle Dandy

               Ch. Jana Zipper

         Ch. Jana Golden Pixie

               Ch. Golden Poppy

               Ch. Teloca Patches Littl' Dickens

         Ch. Lanbur Roshan Hi Fidelity

               Ch. Craigwood's Lucille

Dam: Ch. Lanbur Moonlight 'N Roses

               Ch. Hickorynut Hangman

         Ch. Fairmont Gone With The Wind

               Ch. Pickadilly Pin Up Of Colegren

Ch. Altar's Lanbur Lacey J, thirteen-inch dam of fifteen champions. Owned by Wade Burns and Jon Woodring.

                    Ch. Hickorynuts Hangman
          Ch. Meadow Crest's Grand Slam
                    Ch. Starbuck's Meadow Song
Sire: Ch. Craigwood's Shyster
                    Ch. Swan Lake Spirit of Craigwood
          Ch. Craigwood Savvy
                    Ch. Craigwood's Shannon
                    Ch. Brantwood's Desperado
          Ch. Brantwood Notorious
                    Ch. Craigwood's Shannon
Dam: Ch. Pin Oaks Harpers Bazaar
                    Ch. Rubino's Thumbs Up
          Pin Oaks Sergeant Pepper
                    Ch. Pin Oaks Heavenly Heather

Ch. Bayou Oaks Violetta, fifteen-inch dam of four champions, two of which are BIS winners. Owned by Alyce and Richard Gilmore.

Ch. Starbuck's Full Count

Ch. Keith's Wilkeep Nicodemus

Ch. Wilkeep Love Notes

Sire: Ch. Wilkeep's Bayou Classic

Ch. Wilkeep Music Maker

Ch. Wilkeep Cover Girl

Ch. Wilkeep Hayday Playmate

Ch. Whisper's Call Me Mister

Ch. Whisper's Inflation Fighter

Ch. Suntree's Pucker Pellet

Dam: Ch. Bayou Belladonna

Ch. Cad-Mar's Trix of Starcrest

Woodland Trails Dazzle Doll

Ch. Cad-Mar's Country Morn

Ch. Buglair Belle of Temateki, fifteen-inch dam of nine champions. Owned by Terri Giannetti and Ted Swedalla. *Rick*

                Ch. Pin Oaks Ruffles 'n Ridges

         Ch. Brantwood's Desperado

              Ch. Lokavi's Double Destiny

Sire: Ch. Brantwood Buglair Bandit

                Ch.. Hickorynut Hangman

         Ch. Craigwood's Shannon

              Ch. Craigwood's Lucille

              Ch. Buglair Top Secret

         Ch. Buglair The President

              Buglair Aviatrix

Dam: Buglair Sun Spot

                Ch. Sun Valley's Top Effort

         Ch. Buglair Echo Valley Sunrise

              Ch. Johjean Dawn of Echo Valley

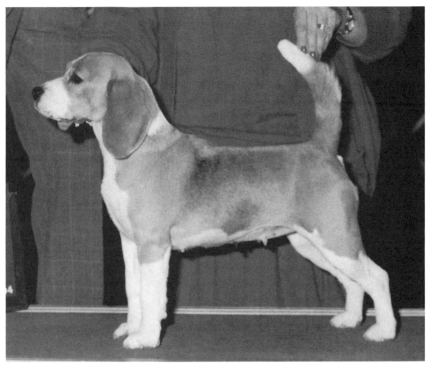

Ch. Echo Run Kindred Spirit, thirteen-inch Group and Specialty winner. Dam of five champions. Owned by John and Peggy Shaw. *Alverson*

                            Ch. Craigwood's Shyster

                  Ch. Craigwood's Wise Decision

                            Ch. Swan Lake's Ric Rac

Sire: Ch. Stonebridge Winning Ways

                            Ch. Craigwood's Murphy

                  Ch. Stonebridge Totally Awesome

                            Ch. Summerhill Cheez Cake

                            Ch. Merry Song's High Point

                  Timberlost's Trapper John

                            Ch. Tarr Hill's Final Curtain

Dam: Ch. Echo Run Shalimar

                            Ch. Touchstone's Smokey Bear CD

                  Ch. Echo Run Heartbreaker

                            Ch. Timberlost Once Is Not Enuf

Ch. Fran Ray's Copper Penny, thirteen-inch dam of twelve champions from four litters. Dam of the Year NBC 1992. Owned by Beverly Newton. *Booth*

                              Ch. Hickorynuts Hangman

                   Ch. Craigwoods Murphy

                            Ch. Craigwood's Lucille

Sire: Ch. Stonebridge Silent Knight

                            Ch. Pixshire's Trouble With Father

                   Ch. Summerhill Cheez Cake

                            Ch. Summerhill Sara Lee

                            Ch. Teloca Patches On Target

                   Ch. Telcoa Patches Littl' Dickens

                            Ch. Teloca Upstage Bann'd 'N Boston

Dam: Ch. Lanbur Sureluv Showboat

                            Ch. Navan's Triple Trouble Rick

                   Ch. Sureluvs Heather Mist

                            Ch. Pixshire's Dark Victress

Ch. Loverly Koala Blue, fifteen-inch dam of six champions. Owned by Liz Rosbach.

```
                        Aust. Ch. Manabay Midas Touch
          Aust., Am. Ch. Torbay Too Hot To Handle
                        Aust., Am. Ch. Torbay Henrietta
Sire: Ch. Manabay Hot Rocks
                        Aust. Ch. Manahound Matchpoint
          Aust. Ch. Manabay Love 'N The Rocks
                        Aust. Ch. Manabay Wun Night Stand
                        Ch. Jana Nassau of Page Mill
          Aust., Am. Ch. Page Mill Oscar
                        Ch. Page Mill Fly By  Night
Dam: Aust. Ch. Manabay Marrietta
                        Aust. Ch. Bandalier Barnabie
          Aust. Ch. Torbay Tamarind
                        Aust. Ch. Annasline Go Jo
```

Ch. Vijam Extraordinaire CD, fifteen-inch dam of nine champions, six in one litter. Owned by Vicky Schultz. *Olson*

               Ch. The Whim's Buckeye

          Ch. Starbuck's Hang 'Em High

               Ch. Elsy's Shooting Star

Sire: Chardon Knockout Punch, C.D.

               Ch. Busch's Gin Rickey

          Ch. Busch's Truly Fair

               Ch. Busch's Black Eyed Susan

               Ch. Chardon Magnific Marathoner

          Ch. Abbey Roads Shot of Brandy

               Lady Abbey Bernhard

Dam: Vijam Extra of Abbey Road

               Ch. Chardon Texas Leaguer

          Vijam Artistry

               Lady Chadsworth Beagle

X-Ander's Miss Blond D, fifteen-inch dam of twenty-four champions. Owned by Jon Woodring and Wade Burns.

Ch. Teloca Patches Littl' Dickens

Ch. Sureluv's Fran Ray's Bandit

Ch. Sureluv's Heather Mist

Sire: Ch. Lanbur Shandell Hit Man

Ch. Craigwood's Murphy

Ch. Stonebridge Lanbur Lady Luck

Ch. Summerhill Cheez Cake

Ch. Teloca Patches Littl' Dickens

Ch. Lanbur Roshan Hi Fidelity

Ch. Craigwood's Lucille

Dam: Ch. Lanbur Shandell High Fasion

Ch. Teloca Patches Littl' Dickens

Ch. Lanbur Sureluv High Society

Ch. Sureluv Summer Mist of Harnett

© ann Mackenzie '88

I n d e x